Glyndebourne
A Celebration

Glyndebourne

A Celebration

edited by John Higgins

JONATHAN CAPE
THIRTY BEDFORD SQUARE LONDON

First published 1984
Reprinted 1984
copyright © 1984 by Jonathan Cape Ltd
Jonathan Cape Limited, 30 Bedford Square, London WC1B 3EL

British Library Cataloguing in Publication Data
Higgins, John, 1934
Glyndebourne.
1. Glyndebourne Festival Opera—History
I. Title
782.1'07'942257   ML38.G63

ISBN 0 224 01905 8

Printed in Great Britain by
Butler & Tanner Ltd,
Frome and London

Contents

v

Illustrations

Illustrations

PLATES

Illustrations

PICTURE CREDITS

The editor and publishers wish to thank Moran Caplat for the loan of pictures for colour plates 2, 7, 8, 10, 11, 12, 14 and 15, and R.J. Crouch for no. 13; and the following for kind permission to reproduce colour photographs: Glyndebourne Festival Opera for nos 1 and 9; Guy Gravett for nos 16–20; and the Victoria and Albert Museum for nos 3–6. For black and white plates, Antony Armstrong-Jones for no. 14; BBC Hulton Picture Library for nos 3–5, 7, 8 and 17; J.W. Derenham for no. 2; Guy Gravett for nos 9–13, 15 and 16, 18–28; Angus MacBean for no. 6; and Twentieth Century Studios for no. 1.

Preface

In the summer of 1984 the Glyndebourne Festival Opera has its fiftieth birthday. The background to the first performances of Mozart there, *Le nozze di Figaro* and *Così fan tutte*, during the late May and early June of 1934, inspired by John Christie, has been described often enough though not always accurately. The most comprehensive account is to be found in Spike Hughes's book, *Glyndebourne, A History of the Festival Opera* (1981).

Few contributors to this book are in a position to recall those pre-war performances. Sir Isaiah Berlin is, of course, the notable exception. So in the main we have concentrated on the post-war years with perhaps an emphasis on the last twenty-five years of Glyndebourne's development. From the start it was decided that the Festival Opera should be viewed both from within and from without. Some essays are written by musicians and directors who have worked, and indeed lived, for lengthy periods in Glyndebourne itself; others come from those who visit it regularly either as members of the paying public or as professional music critics.

Reservations and criticisms are made about Glyndebourne in the following chapters, but doubtless all the contributors will be seen as supporters of the house. And why refute the charge? If we were otherwise we would show a dull lack of concern for the place, we would not make the journey, almost as pilgrims, summer by summer. Nor would we take delight in celebrating this fiftieth birthday.

I would like to express especial thanks to George Christie, Chairman of Glyndebourne, who has been ready with help and advice throughout the preparation of this book and has virtually taken on the role of co-editor; to Brian Dickie, General Administrator of Glyndebourne; to Helen O'Neill for aid on any number of fronts, but above all for the illustrations from the Glyndebourne archives.

London   JOHN HIGGINS
August 1983

My Father's House

George Christie

The founding of a venture such as Glyndebourne in the 1960s or 1970s would, economically, have been suicidal. So, thank heavens my father embarked on his operatic experiment when he did, although it was considered a lunatic enough project at its conception and birth in the 1930s. And, thank heavens, we do not possess the same personality. I don't possess the buccaneer spirit and vision needed to *create* such an opera house.

So things seem to have worked out the right way round – and that, I suppose, is a good reason, with Glyndebourne's continuing survival fifty years after its foundation, why this book is being written.

I was born at Glyndebourne on December 31st, 1934, the same year as the Festival's birth. Even if I did not tread the boards that first year, I was physically, if invisibly, on stage. I have been part of the furniture from the genesis of Glyndebourne's operation and know no other way of life. My parents had the great ambition that, as the only son, I should ultimately assume their mantle. During the war I was evacuated with my mother

I

and sister, Rosamond, to North America. A few months after we arrived there I received a half-size violin from my father and scraped it with my mother's encouragement and with more of her zeal than mine until I grew into playing a full-sized instrument on our return to England in 1944 – and continued to scrape away until 1952. I would go out and buy 78 rpm records of Heifetz and Kreisler and then look for the sheet music (Bach sonatas, Mozart concertos) and play them, where indicated, as fast as my incompetent technique allowed. Even though I was all fingers and thumbs I persisted for another eight years and then forlornly admitted defeat.

I had ambitions to be a singer. I saw in the early years of the Edinburgh Festival, which my father and Rudi Bing (Glyndebourne's General Manager) founded in 1947, many rehearsals and performances. I wanted to be Oscar in *Ballo* and Cherubino in *Figaro* – I was only twelve or thirteen and with an appealing unbroken voice. I sang in the choir and for the Music Society at my school. I took the whole thing quite seriously, and not without some feeling of fulfilment as leader of the choir. Then at a disconcertingly late age my voice broke and my vocal ambitions were snuffed abruptly.

So much for my efforts as an executant musician. But an opera house doesn't *have* to be headed by an *executant* musician – and certainly not by one who persists in the mistaken belief that he is.

My mother died when I was eighteen. She had slaved to keep us alive through the war years in North America – so we saw little of her there. On our return from America towards the end of the war, she began to suffer attacks of migraine and sadly to become increasingly invalid at the time of my adolescence. But I felt a deep attachment to her and since her death have appreciated increasingly and inevitably her penetrating and professional influence in the creation of Glyndebourne.

2

After my mother's death in 1953, my father delegated affairs at Glyndebourne in a selfless way, remaining the figure-head, but generously divesting himself of the day-to-day running of the company. In 1959, when I was particularly 'green' and innocent of the ways of the world, he handed over the chairmanship of the executive company to me – recklessly, it would seem with hindsight. Three years later, and some fifty-two years older than I, he died. I was twenty-seven, had married and in turn just become a father myself.

My parents had been at pains to create a context of inheritance, something which in varying degrees tends to be resisted by an heir. However Glyndebourne, by the time of my father's death, had become an enticing gift-horse for me. It *is* my inheritance. I have become accustomed to this fact – and ardent about it. The context of running an opera company as between 1934, when Glyndebourne was founded, and 1984 has changed massively. The context even between 1962, when my father died, and 1984 has in fact altered almost as much.

For maybe five or more years from settling at Glynde-bourne in 1962 I was a willing passenger, murmuring comments with diffidence from the back-seat. Moran Caplat had been General Manager since 1949 and assumed the role of Prince Regent. He knew the game and had, through the years of Vittorio Gui and Günther Rennert in the 1950s and early 1960s run the 'shop' with vigour and a firm grip.

In the 1960s the way opera in Britain was presented began to develop. Covent Garden under Solti assumed international importance. Scottish Opera took off under Peter Hemmings and Alex Gibson. The Welsh National Opera, originally founded at the start of the 1950s by a beguiling garage proprietor and man of vision, Bill Smith, was gaining in the operatic league tables. And Sadler's Wells Opera was growing out of Islington into the English National Opera at the Coliseum. The competition was for all of us hotting up.

The history of Glyndebourne is in various ways outlined and assessed by the contributors to this book. The milestone personalities in Glyndebourne's past creative history – Fritz Busch and Carl Ebert as artistic parents, Vittorio Gui and Günther Rennert as successors in the 1950s and early 1960s followed by John Pritchard and Franco Enriquez – have in varying degrees of achievement upheld the standards and quality of performance at Glyndebourne. Additionally, Jani Strasser, as a torch-bearer for musical standards in his capacity as head of Musical Preparation from 1934 to 1970, must not be forgotten.

On the 'institutional' side – the part of Glyndebourne by which the artistic operation is made possible – Gerald Coke, Chairman of the Glyndebourne Arts Trust for twenty-four years (almost from the year of its foundation) and a guiding spirit of comprehensive wisdom and understanding, held the 'firm' together and consolidated its strength and objectives.

Since the late 1960s and early 1970s Glyndebourne has grown substantially. I have – with Mary, my wife – become increasingly entangled and identified with Glyndebourne's progress and development. We married at the inadvisable ages of 23 and 21 respectively and settled in the 'big house' in 1962. We repainted a number of rooms and re-upholstered them. In the last years of my father's life Glyndebourne had become 'widowered' and musty. It is still disordered (with the advent over the years of four children) and remains hybrid; but even as the most 'over-used' habitation in England it possesses a certain character of vitality and good-nature. For six months in the year it is overrun by the opera and for the other six months by the family's friends and foibles. The house, in a way, is Glyndebourne's axis. Discard it and its present use, and the whole set-up would be at risk of becoming institutional-ised.

After a burglary here, I received a letter from the thief saying that, if I chose to live in such a large house, I must expect to be a target for his abuse. There seemed to be a strong element of jealousy in his sentiment – and therefore by implication the belief that the house and its contents should be 'anyone's'. A house, like Glyndebourne, must essentially assume in large measure the character and personality of those who live in it. Discard them and (in the case of Glynde-bourne) the way they share it with its operatic partici-pants, and it will become depersonalised – and indeed *'anyone's'*.

It is from this centralised viewpoint that we look out at Glyndebourne's function – rather than, as most do, from the other side of the curtains. And it is from this vantage that we see our participation in the development of Glyndebourne to its present state.

Now, fifty years on, Glyndebourne's base has broadened considerably. It was originally a family affair, financially dependent on the Christies. The Glynde-bourne Arts Trust has gradually, and in recent years substantially, assumed responsibility for the finances of the Company. Sir Anthony Lloyd, an old friend of the family, has succeeded Gerry Coke (who incidentally ought to have been made a peer for his selfless contribu-tion to the Arts and for his success in industry and commerce).

Tony Lloyd who, since taking on chairmanship of the Arts Trust has become ever more eminent in the judicature, has devoted himself to Glyndebourne's well-being. His enthusiasm about its success and his anxiety about any possible threat of failure is truly covetous. He is a pivot around whom Glyndebourne's fortunes spiral upwards. Sir Alex Alexander, the vice-chairman of the Trust, must also be picked out from amongst the other trustees on whom Glyndebourne particularly relies. He has in financial terms simply done more – leagues more – than any other single individual to translate Glyndebourne's fortunes from a state of relative paucity into something approaching financial stability, even vigorous health. He is a man with a Midas touch. But more than anything his particular sense of logic – which he expresses with passion and, where necessary, compassion – about the way in which an enterprise should be run goes to the root of its success.

Brian Dickie has taken over from Moran Caplat. In his first two years as general administrator one or two quite radical changes have been made by him; and the appointment of a number of new people by way of replacements, such as Anthony Whitworth-Jones (who had been the Administrator of the London Sinfonietta and who has now taken over Brian Dickie's previous position), has strengthened Glyndebourne's administration considerably.

Glyndebourne's present repertory has largely been staged by John Cox and Sir Peter Hall, respectively the out-going director of production and the in-coming artistic director. Bernard Haitink, the musical director since 1977, in partnership with Peter Hall, makes the starting-point for the next fifty years look artistically robust.

Many people look at opera with scepticism and pronounce it to be defunct, or at least an anachronism. It needs considerable forces in terms of performers and stage effects, and therefore considerable finance. It has traditionally been subsidised – through the epoch of court opera until today's state or civic opera. Yet it persists as an art form and in terms of popularity is flourishing now perhaps as it has never done before.

6

How odd that this should be, whilst other art forms struggle against the tide of new and competing media. It amazes me that opera still survives in the 1980s. In this context it seems to me that Glyndebourne, as a small-scale operation with an output of two new productions a year and a total repertory averaging five productions spread annually across the Festival and touring operation, as well as other outlets of exploitation, provides the nearest answer today to solvency in opera.

Opera attracts the best talent from the theatre. Carl Ebert became a total convert to opera – as to an important degree his mentor, Max Reinhardt, had been. Peter Hall has wrestled with opera with marked success. Others such as Peter Brook, Patrice Chéreau, John Dexter, Ingmar Bergman have in varying degrees become immersed in opera. And in 1983 Trevor Nunn dipped his toe (or perhaps his leg) in at Glyndebourne with *Idomeneo*.

Conductors are irresistibly drawn from the concert hall to opera. Bernard Haitink, who had done only two operas before he burst on the Glyndebourne scene in 1972, has become unsurpassable in Mozart operas, the Fire and Water test for all conducting in the lyric theatre. Opera has been the stock-in-trade for all the giants of the past – Toscanini, de Sabata, Walter, Furtwängler, Erich Kleiber, Beecham, Busch, and so on – and it continues to suck their successors in.

Glyndebourne as an operatic microcosm – attracting top talent for the top positions, providing the right working context for such talent and confining its output to economically workable proportions – has managed to survive fifty years as virtually the last outpost of private enterprise in opera.

And, unlike my parents, I have four children to choose from, should succession at the end of the twentieth century still be permissible.

A Place for Mozart

Peter Hall

In the 1960s, when I was director of the Royal Shakespeare Company at Stratford, I had a letter from a zealous American which read:

> 'Dear Mr. Hall,
> I am writing a book on the life and works of William Shakespeare and would be grateful for any information you can send me.'

I was appalled by the responsibility. I was similarly appalled when Glyndebourne asked me to write a chapter about Mozart. I can only, however inadequately, try to define what his operas mean to me, as I attempt to understand one of the supreme geniuses.

John Christie built the opera house at Glyndebourne as a place of perfection. The possibility is still there. He dreamt at first of presenting Wagner, but he discovered, once the house was built, that it was Mozart who had found an ideal home in Sussex.

Theatres like certain authors more than others. It took

years of constant refashioning to make the cinema-like art-deco auditorium of Stratford a happy place for Shakespeare. Bayreuth on the other hand, thanks to the composer's understanding of architecture, has always been the best house for Wagner. And in this century, Glyndebourne has blessed Mozart. Why?

Glyndebourne has the right scale for Mozart. He wrote for small theatres, holding only six or seven hundred people. Since his death, opera houses have grown bigger, orchestras have played louder, and the dramatic pretensions of opera have become more grandiose and pompous. Unfortunately, the singers have remained the same size. So the true image of a modern opera production is a super-star singer in a bright follow-spot trying to produce more volume than the virtuoso orchestra. All this is in a huge auditorium before three or four thousand people. Not surprisingly it tends to be an unequal struggle. And even the precise orchestration of Mozart can be coarsened in our new large buildings.

Almost alone among the opera houses constructed in the twentieth century, Glyndebourne was built on the human scale – small enough for the performers' eyes to be seen, their thoughts to be recognised and their inflections understood. Mozart demands this subtlety. Only then can we understand the humanity and wit of his drama. Glyndebourne is small because it was from the first unashamedly elitist, putting quality before quantity. I also suspect that it was difficult to be architecturally grandiose surrounded by the homely proportions of the Sussex Downs.

Glyndebourne is also a community. Artists and technicians meet together for a few months to try to perform an operatic masterpiece. It sounds a simple prescription, but it is one that is rarely followed. It is difficult to indulge in star nonsense at Glyndebourne. In this community, it is the work that matters; and it is the community that is treasured rather than the stars. The stars flourish because they become part of the ensemble, adding to it and being supported by it. Mozart demands ensemble work. His operas require trust and generosity of spirit among the performers. Only then does the delicate interplay of one character with another work – eyes meeting eyes, emotions affecting emotions. So out of Glyndebourne's sense of community has come a unique sense of ensemble. It is an ideal which may not always be achieved in this imperfect world. But it is always aimed at.

Times change and fashions properly change with them. But with John Christie, the ghosts of the two great founding artists of Glyndebourne, Fritz Busch, the conductor and Carl Ebert, the stage director, still inspire the working conditions there. In most opera houses the director is not truly part of the enterprise. He is either a visiting star, bringing a dash of brilliance, if not eccentricity, to the first half-a-dozen performances; or he is a staff director who does the hard work of reviving the piece after the star has gone. In either event, the greater star, the conductor, arrives at the last minute to make his music. By that time his primary concern is that the singers have not been placed anywhere which may impair the sight of his baton.

True opera is action made out of music. And it can only be made by a long, close collaboration between conductor and director, through shared rehearsals. The atmosphere, the action, the character of the drama affect the nature of the music-making. And the music-making affects the drama. Which comes first? Neither. Opera should be a perfect circle, the drama making the music and the music making the drama.

This ideal was established by Busch and Ebert and it is still at the heart of the Glyndebourne tradition. Collaboration creates a healthy sense of ensemble, and is then capable of subtle inflection. There can be no good Mozart unless the conductor and the director combine.

I have worked at Glyndebourne regularly for fourteen years. Bernard Haitink, Raymond Leppard and John Pritchard have joined me in many wonderful journeys. But the most amazing journeys – those which provided the greatest revelation and surprises – have of course been the three operas Mozart wrote with Da Ponte – *Le nozze di Figaro*, *Don Giovanni* and *Così fan tutte*. I have had the good fortune to stage all of them at Glyndebourne, and I have gone on doing them, studying them, and trying to revive my work on them. What, apart from the impossibility of revealing their riches completely, has Glyndebourne taught me about them?

The nineteenth century discovered and developed naturalism in the theatre as a revolutionary force. For the first time, rooms were presented with four walls – though one was removed so that the audience could peep in. Doors and windows were no longer painted on backcloths; they were real, with catches and locks and knobs. This theatre reached its climax with Ibsen and Chekhov; time was 'real', acting tried to be natural behaviour and dialogue pretended to be real speech. The audience, like privileged voyeurs, watched the simulation of life. The vigorous public story-telling of the Greeks and of the Elizabethans, where a character in a play always knows that the audience is watching him and describes his predicament to them in long unreal 'speeches', was no more.

This revolution was very embarrassing for the conventions of opera. Like the old theatre, opera had been based from its beginnings on the convention of public story-telling. In Monteverdi or in Cavalli or even in the *opera seria* of the eighteenth century, a solo aria is always a direct address to the audience. The singer opens his heart to the spectators and always tells the truth to them. (He only dissimulates or tells lies to the other characters.) He reveals himself frankly to the audience as if they were his closest friends. The singer feels his emotions deeply, he also *tells them* then to the audience at exactly the same time. And so he involves them in his predicament.

This ancient narrative acting has a history which takes us all the way back to Homer and to old tribal story-telling. It was of course at the centre of Shakespeare's drama. Hamlet did not come on stage in broad daylight before an audience of three thousand people, many of them fidgeting as they stood, and quietly puzzle to himself about whether or not he should continue to be. He posed the problem for the entire audience and asked their opinion. 'To be or not to be? What do you think?' So Shakespeare uses the soliloquy to hold and involve an audience's attention.

A solo aria works in exactly the same way in Mozart. The mask of public behaviour, of social convention, is taken off. And we see the true heart of the character. Don Ottavio's aria in Act I of *Don Giovanni*, 'Dalla sua pace', was added, I am convinced, not only to please the tenor for the Vienna première, but also to give the audience an early and essential understanding of the true character of the man. Up to this point Don Ottavio has been strong, understanding, helpful – in a way, a surrogate father to the bereaved and neurotic Donna Anna. We may indeed suspect that he is nearly of the same generation as his friend the Commendatore – an entirely suitable match for the great man's daughter. Steady, firm and calm. This aria, always providing that its strong emotions are shared with the audience, shows the inner man. He is not so careful after all. He has a passionate tenderness and an active love for the wayward girl. He becomes, therefore, the positive representative

1 Audrey Mildmay as Zerlina in the pre-war *Don Giovanni*

2 The Act II finale of *Le nozze di Figaro* (1936): Stabile, Rautawaara and Mildmay, Brownlee (*centre*), Nash, Willis and Baccaloni

3   Fritz Busch rehearsing in 1939 while John Christie looks on

4   John Christie with Rudolf Bing in 1939

5 Carl Ebert rehearses Margherita Grandi as Lady Macbeth (1939)

6 Glyndebourne's only wartime production (directed by John Gielgud): Michael Redgrave as Macheath, surrounded by doxies in *The Beggar's Opera* at the Haymarket (1940)

7 Audrey Mildmay with Fritz and
Grete Busch in the Glyndebourne
gardens (1951)

8 The Glyndebourne management,
1951: John Christie on the sofa,
Moran Caplat, Fritz Busch in
conversation with Carl Ebert

of love in the opera – a strong moral character, well able
to match the God-testing evil of Giovanni.

If Don Ottavio sings this aria to himself as a positive
reflection of something he already knows, the effect may
be romantic in a generalised sort of way. But the specific
action of the aria, the amazement we should feel at
seeing his mask removed, at seeing the strong man
underneath, is lost. And a crucial part of our understanding of the character is lost also.

Solo arias in Mozart are always concerned with the
revelation of the character's true feeling, with the
unashamed removal of the mask. The action of every
aria is a revelation of self.

Since naturalism swept our theatre, opera as well as
drama has become frightened of this honest exposure.
Singers go to great lengths to ignore their audiences, and
to pretend that their arias are private communings with
themselves. The true drama of the aria is therefore
betrayed.

The need for this public demonstration of the heart is
even greater when we come to the ensembles – those
great and unique glories of Mozart's operas. Unfortunately, naturalism has damaged our appreciation of them
also.

Singers in ensembles either stand rooted to the spot,
carefully blending together as if the drama were over and
the concert had begun; or they desperately bend the text
so that half sing the same line *to* each other in happy
agreement – anything to avoid the direct address to the
audience. And this communication is the heart of the
great ensemble. Musically, a proper ensemble demands
a sense of balance, of blend. No singer must out-sing the
others. But he must, if the drama is to work, try to out-
act the others.

In Act IV of *Figaro*, Cherubino flirts in the darkness of
the garden with the figure that he believes to be

Susanna. Actually, it is the Countess who has disguised herself as Susanna in an attempt to catch her own husband. Unknown to them, they are observed by Figaro, Susanna and the Count. These three are unaware of the presence of each other. At this point of rich complexity, the Countess, Susanna, Figaro and the Count all sing the same text to the audience, believing, each one of them, that they are the only person speaking:

> 'Se il ribaldo ancor sta saldo,
> La faccenda guasterà'
> (If the scoundrel stays any longer
> he'll ruin everything)

All four characters have very different emotional states. The Count is full of jealousy for Cherubino, because he sees his assignation with Susanna disappearing. Figaro expresses blacker jealousy: he sees his plot to catch his wife with the Count about to be wrecked by Cherubino – whose attentions to his wife are, incidentally, not repulsed as strongly as he would like. The Countess is distraught because she sees her plot about to be ruined by the recklessly flirtatious Cherubino. Discovery is imminent. And Susanna, not for the first time on this mad day, sees with her usual unblinking clarity, that the ice is in danger of breaking. All their lives are about to be wrecked.

All this is expressed at once in a short section of the ensemble. Mozart is using a device which is unique to opera. If four people speak at once in a play, the result is incoherent. Even if their speech is drilled with the precision of a dance team, the effect is abstract and inhuman. But in opera, and particularly in Mozart's operas, we can look at each one of the four characters for a split second, and then move on to the next, comparing their differing attitudes, contrasting their differing emotions. We listen to the same text from each of them, but we understand the rich irony in their differing inflections. Only opera can deal coherently with emotions and words of several people at once. And for us, the audience, it is a moment of chaos made clear. The music gives it shape and form.

Glyndebourne as a place has made me understand that the whole of Mozart's drama is based on a performer's ability to speak directly to his audience. It is at that moment that he removes his mask. And Mozart's theatre is very much about the mask. This preoccupation with illusion and reality, with social lies and emotional truth, leads to the constant preoccupation of Da Ponte and Mozart with impersonation. Leporello disguises himself as Don Giovanni and is credible enough to seduce the hapless Elvira. The Countess disguises herself as Susanna and is credible enough to deceive her own husband. Guglielmo and Ferrando in *Così fan tutte* disguise themselves as foreign officers in order to find out which girl they love. By disguising themselves, they find themselves.

These disguises must be taken extremely seriously and not treated as facetious devices of the theatre. Leporello has to be the same size and shape as Don Giovanni – otherwise the love scenes with Elvira simply become the excesses of *buffo* theatre. Even worse, the chromatic anguish of Elvira at the beginning of Act II becomes a way of provoking farcical laughs as Leporello serenades her. Susanna and the Countess must credibly change persons. The people who are deceived must be well deceived.

There is some evidence that Mozart's original singers enjoyed the vocal problem of disguising their voices so that they also *sounded* like the people they were representing. It was obviously a theatrical effect well liked by the audience and well done by the performer. It is disturbing as well as amusing. Nowadays it is hardly even attempted.

All this role playing is of course revolutionary. If a Count can become a servant, and a servant become a Count, rank itself is questioned. I believe that Mozart and Da Ponte were out to show that man with his clothes off, man in the bedroom, is much the same animal whether he be aristocrat or peasant. A man's clothes do not make the man – it is his heart that matters. The French Revolution is just over the horizon.

Artistically as well as politically, Mozart was writing at a moment which we can now see as a watershed of history – a key moment of change. Like Shakespeare, who was equally fortunate, he inherited a perfectly tuned, perfectly proportioned classical tradition. Without the form of Elizabethan verse, without Marlowe, without Kyd, without Spenser, Shakespeare could never have modulated blank verse into his uniquely human instrument. The irregularities of the rhythm, and the unexpected changes in the scansion give life to the classical lines. It was the same for Mozart. He inherited the perfect form, the perfect pattern and the perfect grammar of classical music. The eighteenth century, the world of Enlightenment, knew what music was. Mozart's chromaticism, his shifts of key, his sudden breaking of the rules, not only point the way to Beethoven and the romanticism of the nineteenth century; they express the anguish of humanity in a classical setting. The mask is off here as well. Life is expressed by change.

It is difficult for us to remember now how casually Mozart was regarded even eighty years ago. He was the decorator, the charming tinkling boy of the eighteenth century. Glyndebourne since the 1930s has done much for Mozart. *Idomeneo* has been discovered for the English; *Così fan tutte* has been revalued. And from Busch to Haitink there have been decades of immaculate musical performances. Audiences come to Glyndebourne for Mozart. And singers come to Glyndebourne to learn their Mozart. Scholarship and style are highly prized at Glyndebourne. It is a tradition started by the late Jani Strasser, who was head of the music staff, and is today carried on by Martin Isepp.

But it is a paradox of our time that while the fashion for 'authenticity' grows, so the freedom of the director to be unauthentic – to ignore stage directions, or the period specified by the composer – grows also. It is difficult of course to speak of 'authenticity' for staging. It must necessarily be a limited ideal because the modern audience is different, and in no sense has the same understanding, prejudices, or preoccupations as the original audience. It follows therefore that even if we had all the knowledge, we could not make a reproduction work. But knowledge of the original performance conditions undoubtedly helps us understand how we can communicate to our own audiences.

Glyndebourne has often made me think about the original conditions that Da Ponte and Mozart worked under. Their theatre was filled with lighted candles and there was almost as much light on the audience as on the performers. The communion between them must therefore have been complete – certainly better than we have in our days of electricity and huge darkened auditoriums.

Mozart had other great benefits which we can learn from and try to reproduce. In a candle-lit theatre, when Figaro walks on and announces that it is very, very dark, the audience accept the fact. From then on they will imagine that it *is* dark. They can understand and appreciate all the mistaken identities of Act IV of *Figaro* because, unlike the characters pretending that they are in the dark, the audience can still see. By the light of that even candle-power they can understand what the characters are feeling. In the literal naturalism of our electrically-lit theatres, we are always expected to make darkness, because, at the switch of a dimmer, we *can* make darkness. If Figaro tells us it is dark in a modern opera house, we expect all the lights to be very dim. But in this naturalistic gloom, it is impossible to follow the plot or the emotions because we cannot see.

The problem is enormous because darkness is a central obsession of Da Ponte's. It is a time for mistaken identities, for sensualities, for revolution. Elvira needs darkness in Act II in *Don Giovanni* if she is to break our hearts. Act IV of *Figaro* is impossible unless we believe in the velvet darkness of that very sensual night. Glyndebourne at least allows us a degree of darkness which would be impractical in a larger house. We can still see.

What else can we learn from the beginnings of these masterpieces? We know that in Mozart's day, pitch was about a semitone lower. We also know that the orchestral sound must have been generally quieter – because eighteenth-century instruments had nothing like the attack or sonority of their modern counterparts. They were the right accompaniment for Mozart's generation of singers. Nancy Storace, the original Susanna, was seventeen when she created the role. The first Don Giovanni was just twenty-three. We must therefore imagine young fresh voices supported by a delicate texture of sound. Da Ponte complains about many things, but he never complains that his words cannot be heard. With a man of his verbal precision and wit, words must have been very important. They still are.

I suspect that Mozart would have been delighted by the virtuosity and size of our modern orchestras – just as he was delighted by the Mannheim orchestra. It is clear that the technical standards of instrumental playing have improved beyond all recognition. But I wonder whether Mozart – and Da Ponte also – would have liked the large voices that we now need to ride over the huge volume of sound. Or the fashion among many modern singers to suppress their consonants in order to preserve the shape of the vocal line. I doubt therefore whether things have improved generally. Delicacy, precision, real *piano*, real *pianissimo* and a relish for the words were the necessary objectives then – and they seem even harder to achieve now.

The three Da Ponte operas are about the pain of love – and specifically about the anguish occasioned by sexual attraction. The pain and the anguish are in the music. The erotic atmosphere is there too – but it is also of course in the words. Only the English Restoration dramatists – Wycherley, Congreve or Dryden – can rival Da Ponte's love of *double-entendre*. I sometimes think that these sly obscenities were slipped in to make Mozart giggle as he composed. Are the characters aware of the implications of what they are saying or not? Generally I think they are. Susanna's delightful anxiety about the 'pini' where the assignation is to occur is a humorous release for her anxieties over the whole plot. These characters are not mealy-mouthed; there is no nineteenth-century prudishness – rather an appreciation of the funniness as well as the pain of sex.

But having considered the words we must go back to the music. Mozart is a great dramatist because the atmosphere, the action, and the character of the drama are all expressed by the orchestra. If the performers listen to the orchestra, know the orchestration, they will know what their characters are doing. The score of *Figaro* for instance, contains a continuous commentary on the failings, the weaknesses and the anguish of the characters. Horns bray and mock as Figaro contemplates cuckoldry; woodwinds chatter away in irony to deflate the Count's pomposity; warm clarinets show the sensuality and directness of Susanna.

All this is a wonderful gift to the singer. The orchestra has only to be used. In the right state of physical relaxation (a lesson that the great Callas showed to operatic actors) the orchestra can seem to well out of the performer's body. He is filled with the richness of its sound, its contradictions, its chromatic surprises, and does not have to illustrate these matters by moving in time to the music or making huge gestures in a vain attempt to match a climax. In the right state of relaxation, an entire Mozartian orchestra can be working for the singer.

All this is easier to achieve at Glyndebourne. Many of us – artists and audiences – have reason to be grateful that in Glyndebourne, England has found a place for Mozart.

The Strauss Operas

John Cox

On May 28th, 1959 the curtain rose upon the first Glyndebourne production of *Der Rosenkavalier*. Originally contemplated as early as 1935, it finally arrived in time to celebrate the company's twenty-fifth anniversary. In 1984 it will be joined in the Glyndebourne story by its sister *Arabella* in celebration of the fiftieth. (Oddly, neither anniversary has been marked by a new Mozart production!) Between whiles Strauss has assumed an importance second to Mozart himself in the Glyndebourne repertoire, with Rossini the only close rival, and it has been my pleasurable task to be closely associated with this development, almost from the start.

I was very fortunate indeed in 1959, my first year at Glyndebourne, to be assistant to Carl Ebert on *Der Rosenkavalier*. The creative team of Ebert, Oliver Messel and Leopold Ludwig combined with the soprano trio of Crespin, Söderström and Rothenberger to produce a quite unforgettable account of this great masterpiece. The grand opera tradition by which it had been taken over and seriously compromised was firmly swept aside.

Here instead, in intimate surroundings, was the original music drama; and here in consequence was an intimation of what the future held for Strauss and Glyndebourne; for, notwithstanding its undoubted moments of great ceremony, surface extravagance and startling farce, here was domestic comedy. This is perhaps Strauss's happiest creative vein, one which certainly coincides most nearly with Glyndebourne's *genius loci*.

Capriccio was next in 1963. With *Ariadne auf Naxos*, first presented in 1950, as a well established favourite, it seemed that these three would complete Glyndebourne's exploration of the Strauss canon, and his importance waned until 1971, when a new production of *Ariadne auf Naxos* was followed in quick succession by another *Capriccio* and the addition of *Intermezzo* and *Die schweigsame Frau* to the family. These four operas are the principal subject of this study, forming themselves naturally into a group sharing to a greater or lesser extent the world of professional music and theatre as a theme. Each has a strong domestic element also and I suggest that, in yoking together these two preoccupations, the domestic and the professional, Strauss gives us an exceptionally rich and accurate autobiography.

Clearly *Der Rosenkavalier* and *Arabella* fall outside this concept. I cannot leave the former, however, without first citing the figure of Octavian as an ancestor to much of what was to come. Octavian, in rejecting the seigneurial promiscuity of Ochs to embrace a romantic monogamy with Sophie, assumes a central position in Straussian orthodoxy, for from this point onwards Strauss seldom misses an opportunity to proclaim the supremacy of marriage over all other relationships. His own marriage was famous; and the many who, perhaps wishfully, imagine a libertine future for the young Octavian would find no support from Strauss. Furthermore, and in spite of the non-professional context, Octavian is arguably

Strauss's first portrait of a theatrical individual. We are accustomed to perceiving the Composer in the 'Vorspiel' to *Ariadne* as derivative in type from Octavian; yet it is more instructive to reverse the standpoint and make a study of Octavian not, admittedly, as a composer, but as an actor of great creative flair. The clue is already there in the opening scene with the Marschallin – no *post coitum triste* here, nor even a restorative nap; instead an energetically verbose analysis of roles in their relationship, during which the Marschallin is reduced to a bemused audience of one. It is later Octavian's notion entirely to disguise himself as a maid, *his* choice to remain in the room with Ochs, accepting the challenges of the new role instead of taking any of the excellent chances created by the Marschallin to leave. The consequences which flow from this embody the structure of the opera, and in Act III Mariandl has to produce a *tour de force* of improvised dramatic art. In addition, we must note the superbly accomplished performance required of Octavian in the presentation of the rose, where again he assumes centre stage with the perfect aplomb that comes from the pronounced super ego of a born actor. Add to this his engagement in Valzacchi of a producer to deal with setting, costume, script and supporting actors and Octavian's credentials are complete: a theatrical portrait to rank with the Composer, Henry Morosus and La Roche to mention only the most prominent.

Richard Strauss was born in Munich, but operatically he belonged to Dresden; for of his fourteen operas no fewer than nine received their first performance there. Dresden had a long and distinguished tradition of treating opera as drama, dating back at least as far as Weber (who among other matters paid particular attention to lighting!) and thus provided a natural home for the complex theatrical demands of Strauss's work. This association, exclusive from *Feuersnot* until *Der Rosenkavalier*, was then broken for *Ariadne auf Naxos* and *Die Frau ohne Schatten*, only to be resumed with *Intermezzo*. This last was conducted by Fritz Busch, who so delighted Strauss that he gave him the première of his next opera and made him the co-dedicatee of the one after, *Arabella*, with the intention that he should conduct its first performance also.

However, by this time it was 1933 and events were in motion which would lead to the scattering of many great artistic partnerships. Busch was utterly unacceptable to the new Nazi government, and indeed it to him. He was dismissed. But Strauss was held to his contract and not permitted to withdraw *Arabella* in protest, while Busch left Germany for ever.

On the night of February 12th, 1945 Dresden with its opera house was destroyed by British and American bombs. Happily, if ironically, the seeds of its great operatic tradition, planted by Busch, had rooted securely in the unlikely soil of Sussex, for Glyndebourne was already ten years old. Moreover, the friendship between Strauss and Busch, however tested by their divergent fates at Nazi hands, was sufficiently enduring for Busch to see the potential of the intimate Sussex opera house as a suitable home for Strauss music drama in the Dresden tradition.

Early discussion centred on *Der Rosenkavalier* in a specially reduced orchestration, but alas neither lived to see the realisation of this dream in 1959. However, if Strauss had visited Glyndebourne before the war he would certainly have seen it as a natural home for another of his pieces, yet to be written. Stefan Zweig had urged him to examine the Abbé Casti's text, 'Prima la musica e poi le parole', later to become his final opera *Capriccio* and using a setting not dissimilar to that of

Glyndebourne. Here, incredibly enough for post-depression Europe, was a wealthy patron possessed of an ancestral home with a music room and a theatre, making arrangements in the middle of the countryside for the most elegantly informal performances of the highest standard. *Capriccio* was given its première in Munich at the height of the war, not long before its opera house too was destroyed by bombs. At that time the chasm between our two countries must have seemed likely to be eternally unbridgeable, yet today *Capriccio* is more at home at Glyndebourne than at almost any other opera house. Performances of it have an absolute rightness of location there, while rehearsals always possess that exceptional amalgam of ease and intensity which is both Glyndebourne's unique gift to the artist and the special characteristic of the opera itself.

There has only been one Countess in all four seasons that *Capriccio* has been performed at Glyndebourne: Elisabeth Söderström who, from her first appearance in 1957, has been closely associated with the progress of Richard Strauss there. Her portrayals of the Composer, Octavian and Christine Storch surely demand comparison with Lotte Lehmann. As Countess Madeleine in *Capriccio*, however, she is enthroned unchallengeably as the composer's undoubted Muse.

Capriccio was first produced by Günther Rennert in 1962, with sets by Dennis Lennon and costumes by Anthony Powell. Söderström was doing her first Countess, and relates wryly that on the first day of rehearsal Rennert had told her, 'This opera fails with the Countess'. I remember finding the production as sharp and meticulous as all Rennert's work, but quite glacial, and I think I was justified in sensing that Rennert did not love the piece. When Moran Caplat asked me to do a new production in the old designs for 1973 it was part of my first three-year 'package' as Director of Production, whereby in exchange for one new production (*Intermezzo*) I agreed to a series of compromises, which producers usually detest so much. As it turned out, two of these were amongst my most satisfying productions at Glyndebourne. One was *La Bohème* and the other *Capriccio*.

It so happened that the Munich company were visiting Covent Garden in March 1972 with *Capriccio* in their repertoire. I was left fascinated by it but unmoved and was now very perturbed by the fact that two fine productions of this opera could thus fail to engage me. It soon occurred to me that this opera, perhaps more than any other, needed to be released from its trappings, for the elaborate rococo of the prescribed setting, instead of delivering the work, in fact masked it.

The central issue in *Capriccio*, whether music is superior to poetry, or vice versa, can happily never be resolved. The conflict is neatly embodied in the rival suits of a composer and a poet to the Countess. She, not wishing to lose one love by choosing the other, proposes opera as a way to the best of both worlds. This compromise, far from being a solution, sharpens a conversational topic into a vexed confrontation, for in opera the rivalry between words and music is enacted with every performance. Those who work in opera are inevitably caught up in the struggle.

Capriccio is a conversation piece, concerned with ideas. Given that the issues are as alive today as they ever were, that by performing the opera at all we are contributing to the argument, I wanted to find a way to do it that would stress its contemporaneity. The other productions I had seen, perhaps because of the opera's static nature, had lent the proceedings the air of a museum. I wanted to portray a number of professional artists discussing their work with their patrons, but periwigs, paniers, breeches and buckles can so easily trap the issues in a bygone age.

26

Bringing it right up to date, however, would have been untrue to another aspect of the work, for the social circumstances of *Capriccio* are not of the present. The task was thus to find a time as close as possible to our own which would work at this level.

Paris in the decade after the First World War had all that was needed. Patronesses like the Princesse de Polignac commissioned work from Stravinsky, Cocteau, Les Six and others for private consumption. All of these were concerned with problems of form, many with finding new ways of combining words and music for the theatre. Diaghilev and Reinhardt bestrode the theatrical scene.

Most of all, the post-war relaxation in style of social behaviour, with its ingenious emphasis on comfort with elegance, accords well with Strauss's music. It also releases to the performer a rich vocabulary of gesture, posture and moment-to-moment activity which is more accessible to both audience and actors, being much closer to their own, and which can only assist in pointing the relevance of the conversation to us as we watch.

La Roche, the producer, is anxious to people the stage with 'creatures of flesh and blood', people like ourselves with whom we can all identify. My interpretation of *Capriccio* was an attempt to please him.

The first Strauss opera to be essayed by Glyndebourne was *Ariadne auf Naxos*. Here, too, the presence in the story of a wealthy patron, a private house and a specially ordered performance give a happy resonance to the proceedings. Glyndebourne can even, with no fear of holocaust, actually present the firework display alluded to by the Major Domo as the audience leaves, although on one famous occasion this was suspended for the season when the gamekeeper protested that all the new pheasant chicks had died of fright. In subsequent years 'bangers' were banned and 'whooshers' now reign supreme.

I don't agree with those who hold that the first version, with the play preceding the opera, is superior. Sir Thomas Beecham was, I believe, one such and he conducted the Glyndebourne première for the Edinburgh Festival in 1950. I worked as assistant on the revival of this in 1962 in a perfectly good presentation by a company of actors, singers and dancers of all-round distinction. It is not any weakness of the play with music of version I, but the supreme quality of the 'Vorspiel' of version II which settles the argument. Strauss, in resisting Hofmannsthal's blandishments to compose that 'Vorspiel' said, 'I have an innate antipathy to all artists treated in plays and novels, and especially composers, poets and painters'. Yet in this masterly composition he depicts an accurate, ironic, loving picture of professional back-stage life which is crowned by his portrait of the young composer, one of his supreme creations.

Perhaps it is natural for those who devote their lives to the imaginary portrayal of princes, priests, prostitutes and politicians on the stage to react over-enthusiastically to a chance to reveal their own world. Certainly, when approaching the new production of *Ariadne auf Naxos* in 1971 I felt that the sharpness of the Strauss–Hofmannsthal picture of theatrical life was blurred by setting it in a large room, as suggested in the score. With Glyndebourne itself as a cue, I proposed to Michael Annals that we should set the 'Vorspiel' back-stage. He in turn, with a stroke of quite characteristic genius, said, 'Why not under the stage?' and one of the most satisfying settings I have ever had the pleasure of using was all but ready! Moran Caplat, who had a gratifying habit of spotting a winning idea and doubling his stake, sent us off to Stockholm to see the eighteenth-century court theatre at Drottningholm. The visit was a revelation. In the autumn stillness of that empty old theatre, the great wheel under the stage slumbered in its cradle of ropes. These strained in all directions towards other wheels which in turn connected to slots and slides and traps serving the scene changes above. Here indeed was a most rewarding setting for the 'Vorspiel', with its rival teams swarming as busily as ants among the technical paraphernalia of theatrical creativity, almost crushed by the weight of the impending opera overhead.

The resultant design was generally accounted a success, whereas that for the opera itself which follows raised doubts. Again, the scenic prescription of Hofmannsthal could be questioned. Why put Ariadne *outside* a cave when, by putting her inside, one could clearly represent her captivity in a fateful obsession. How much more poignant to see her sitting at the mouth of the cave looking out to sea for her deathly lover. How telling to see the bowsprit of his swiftly arriving ship thrust into the cave, eventually to burst it asunder and release her! I still stand by this concept and do not regret the lack of 'prettiness' which upset some colleagues and critics. Certainly the function of the *commedia dell'arte* troupe came as welcome and colourful relief, exactly as M. Jourdain would have wanted. I was fortunate always in this group – carefully chosen each time and disposing as decisively as possible of all the old sweeping nonsense about opera singers not being able to act. This singing, acting, dancing, miming, masking group performed every aspect of their art at the highest degree of precision and so created by their skill the possibility of making ever greater demands. It was a supremely satisfying experience working on their scenes.

The decision to add *Intermezzo* to the Glyndebourne repertoire in 1974 was the occasion for some misgiving. Strauss lovers tend to mark it low for musical quality, and besides, hardly anyone had ever seen it, even in Germany. All that was generally known about this work was its autobiographical nature, which had laid Strauss open to charges of tastelessness, its frequent shifts of scene (including an accident on a toboggan run), and the fact that Elisabeth Söderström was aching to play the lead. This final positive easily outweighed all the negatives and work duly began on what was to become perhaps the most surprising public success of the whole Strauss repertoire at Glyndebourne.

This was in no small part due to its performance in English. At the time, Glyndebourne was going through a phase of performances in translation. *The Cunning Little Vixen* from the Czech was uncontroversial; in the case of *The Visit of the Old Lady* the composer Von Einem's insistence that it should be understood by the audience won the day. However, with *Intermezzo*, here was a German opera by an immortal. Would this be the thin end of the wedge? Strauss himself was our most important ally here in the case for translation. He clearly, and I believe, justifiably fancied himself in the unfamiliar role of librettist and had, in his lengthy foreword to the opera, placed heavy insistence on the audibility of the text. And if the text must be heard, then logically it must be understood. The compositional style, too, gives greater freedom to translation, for here once more in a highly developed state is the manner of the *Ariadne* 'Vorspiel', with its rapid and easy alternation of secco recitative, accompagnato, plain speech and lyric effusion. Söderström, too, was anxious to have the audience understand her. With a text full of jokes, outrageous tantrums, rapid changes of mood and mind, sentiment and irony she saw the role of Christine as a gift for an actress, an opportunity to deploy every weapon in her formidable but perhaps under-exploited armoury as a comedienne. Her English is fortunately impeccable as is

that of Marco Bakker, the Dutch baritone cast opposite
her. So Moran Caplat finally agreed to performance in
the vernacular – provided the translator was the best
available. At that time, and perhaps still today, that
could only mean Andrew Porter, who was in Sydney for
the opening of the new opera house. A cable to the
Antipodes secured the required answer only nine months
before rehearsals began. Andrew joined the company for
some days during these and responded with sympathetic
vigour to the comparatively few problems which the
translation was presenting, altering or defending, everywhere polishing, to achieve an outstanding result.

The autobiographical nature of *Intermezzo* is a clear
invitation to do a production as an exercise in Strauss
archaeology. This was turned down at once, principally
because I believe that the piece has an inner strength
and truth which enables it to transcend its initial
données. Strauss himself was evidently very keen to
underline its personal nature in the first production, yet
it is still the case that he refers throughout the score to
'The Wife' and 'The Husband', as if to imply some
claim to universality. This claim must surely be allowed,
for *Intermezzo* goes beyond the minutiae of its events to
achieve a very recognisable study of the strains on a
marriage when challenged and rivalled by the pressures
of a major career involving long separations. By de-
Straussifying the tale we were able to adopt freedoms
from which even he, for all his boldness, would have
flinched. Setting the opening scene in their bedroom
rather than his dressing room, for instance, it was
possible to imply that a fulfilled love life was what the
wife would miss most of all during the husband's
absence, hence giving her animosity a very credible
neurotic undertone.

The design of the show, with its succession of short,
concentrated scenes, was of paramount importance. It

should come across as a series of pictures in a scrap-book, each one telling its story with immediate impact at a glance, each one somehow slightly different in flavour, colour, focus even, and with a surprise on every page. In the previous year Martin Battersby had created the costumes and furniture for the new 'twenties' *Capriccio*, and he was the obvious choice as designer. Until his untimely death in 1982 he was amongst the top world experts on Art Nouveau and Art Deco, and his collections and books devoted to these periods of fine art history have secured his fame for posterity. This reputation, however, masked his training and experience as a stage designer, and in *Intermezzo* he was able to bring both sides of his talent into focus. His unerring eye for detail, his careful scholarship and his sense of theatrical values achieved a bravura display of vignettes, most memorably the projections during the orchestral intermezzi. Picking up on the idea of a scrap-book narrative, he invented for these a series of 'newspaper photographs' illustrative of the action. They were done by a process of hand-dotted 'daguerrotype', each measuring at least twelve by nine inches, which took him hours and hours of patient labour. They were themselves superb works of art. For them, and for the wonderful way in which he designed for Söderström, I shall always remember him.

As for the lady herself, she seized every opportunity offered by the role. It was a memorable display of emotional and physical versatility, in which everything required of her – whether reading a newspaper, falling off a toboggan or donning a deep cloche hat – was performed with generous comic artistry. As for the famous nagging, which seems to be about all that the world at large remembers of Pauline Strauss, Söderström delivered this with the sharpness that stimulates rather than draws blood. Its erotic message was subtle but potent, and certainly revealed the secret of this otherwise inexplicably happy marriage. It is a pleasure to record that in the 1983 revival of this production, Felicity Lott's portrayal of Christine was adjudged a triumph; Söderström herself saw a performance and joined in the general enthusiasm.

In *Die schweigsame Frau* Strauss also touches on the subject of an operatic marriage in which the absurdity of taking a singer to wife is grounds sufficient for one of the characters to be disinherited! Here he was able to poke fun at much that he loved most dearly – marriage, music, singers, operatic convention, even, affectionately, many of his great forebears in frequent musical pastiche. Strauss really adored Stefan Zweig's libretto, and lavished the most hyperbolic praise on it. If in the end the piece seems a thought heavy-handed compared with the Hofmannsthal repertoire, this must be attributed to the idolatry in which its two creators held each other.

The central problem for me in approaching this work was quite literally the suspension of disbelief. How can this life of a man who hates loud noise be depicted by a full Strauss orchestra, and how is it that such a man can spend so much time shouting at people?

Further, two decisions by Zweig in his adaptation of Ben Jonson's play for the libretto are baffling. First, Jonson had the sagacity to furnish Morosus with a mute servant who had a rich line in sign language; Zweig prefers a talkative Marcellina type whose employment should not have lasted five minutes. Secondly, and sadly, he does away with Jonson's central situation implied in its subtitle *Epicoene*, whereby the old man's silent wife turns out to be a boy actor in disguise. Here surely was a golden opportunity for Strauss to introduce a travesti role, this time with central dramatic justification. Perhaps by that point in European social history sexual ambiguity had become too disreputable for it ever again to be found as 'delightful' as before the First World War.

The case for performing the opera in English was strong, based as it is on Ben Jonson, set in London, with plentiful Englishry in the text as well as much dialogue, and a score not redolent of melody. We did indeed set out with that in mind. However, the reason why we did it in German was because the vocal demands of the three principal roles are so taxing that one must shop in world markets to cast it at all and few first-class singers will take the trouble to learn infrequently performed operas in any other language than the original.

Probably the characteristic which stands in the way of *Die schweigsame Frau* becoming a popular piece is its unrelenting attempt to use cruelty as a comic resource. The opera got Strauss into some trouble with the newly ensconced Hitler government as he stood up for his revered but Jewish librettist, yet it contains disturbing elements which might otherwise have appealed to the Nazis. Here is brutality as a means of persuasion; here is persecution as a method of imposing conformity, blithely provided by a writer who was to become one of the diabolical regime's most distinguished victims. In the end, it is hard to enjoy the joke or to accept the glib reconciliation which seems to be based on the dangerous principle that technique triumphs over truth – a dubious lesson for art to be propounding at that or any other time.

This brilliant but disturbing work was Strauss's third study of the theatrical life. With *Capriccio* still to come, it was already a formidable total for the composer who had expressed such a distaste for depicting the artist on stage. The 'Vorspiel' to *Ariadne* is the first to look at theatrical people, their weaknesses, ambitions and compromises exposed; sorting out their relationships with each other, their public and their art. In *Intermezzo* the theme achieves its most personal expression in the portrait of a show-business marriage under pressure. *Die schweigsame Frau* presents the harshest portrait of all of the theatrical profession, where performance in service of the imagination is replaced by that in pursuit of a lie.

Fortunately this was not the composer's last word. In *Capriccio* he sums up a lifetime of practical wisdom about the artist and his most vital creative relationships – with partner, interpreter, impresario, patron, public and finally, in Madeleine's great closing monologue, with himself. *Capriccio* must be amongst the most deeply thought and felt theatrical statements about the theatre that has ever been written, and its intellectual force is suffused with a love, respect and gratitude for music drama which serve to dignify all who work in it.

The Baroque Operas

Raymond Leppard

Glyndebourne began with Mozart and for years that composer was regarded, not without reason, as the company's speciality. But it was really the special qualities of the place, the people there and the attitude towards rehearsal that made things go so well and persuaded public opinion to that conclusion. The house certainly pioneered Mozart in England, but, by the time the war was ended, everyone played his operas, standards of ensemble were sometimes nearly as good as in Sussex and the standards of singing sometimes better. What remained to sustain Glyndebourne's particularity was the liberality of spirit, engendered by its founder, which pervaded the whole organisation. John Christie understood that, outside Glyndebourne, changes had come about and gave every encouragement for his company to experiment and find another 'speciality' beside Mozart that would maintain Glyndebourne's reputation.

At first, largely due to the enthusiasm of Vittorio Gui, it was Rossini who was chosen to share the course, and he ran a good race. But soon his operas, too, began to be played everywhere. It is tempting to come to the conclusion that there is nothing so contagious as operatic quality, but something closer to 'follow my leader' would seem to have been the name of the game. In any case, the Rossini vein continued successfully for some years until its particularity was dissipated. Other styles had, by this time, been introduced but none had established a new speciality for the company.

Then, far ahead of its time, Glyndebourne struck out again and in 1962 mounted the first fully professional performance of Monteverdi's *L'incoronazione di Poppea* in England, some 280 years after its first performance in Venice.

Only a few days after the first performance John Christie died. His son, George, had already been Chairman of the Board since 1959 and the spirit of confident adventure persisted quite undiminished by the change in leadership. It was, nevertheless, fitting that the founder should have lived until this latest 'speciality' was initiated.

It was a risky venture for Glyndebourne and this is how it came about. While I was a student at Cambridge I had become obsessed by the immense power of Monteverdi's music. His name had been accorded traditional respect in music history lectures, but it was not based on any certain knowledge of his work. Believe it or not, even in that august seat of learning, the Pendlebury music library in 1948 boasted, if my memory serves me, only two volumes of the Malipiero complete (at that time, admittedly, incomplete) edition and a few madrigals scattered among some heavily edited collections of German origin. The reality of Monteverdi's music was not readily available either in print or performance.

I was lucky enough to have become a member of the Cambridge University Madrigal Society. Its conductor,

Boris Ord, was enthusiastic about the small number of Monteverdi's madrigals that he knew. Having spent part of his early professional life as a repetiteur in Cologne, he clearly sensed the theatricality of them, and we performed them often. For me they were a revelation. I had never heard music like it, let alone taken part in the performing of it. The directness of the music's response to the meaning of the words, even within the somewhat restricting medium of the five-voiced madrigal, was to me astounding and the need to explore this unique world of musical expression became paramount. In succeeding years as I moved out into the professional world (which included two seasons on the music staff at Glyndebourne) I began to put concerts of his music together including, naturally enough, excerpts from his operas. *L'incoronazione di Poppea* especially fascinated me. It seemed the epitome of a style which set out to convey to the listener the emotional import of words with a directness that involved every aspect of their presentation; singing, playing, acting, delivery and accompaniment. No one could sit back uninvolved in this music without betraying it. The highly sensuous plot and the libretto which expounded it gave composer and performers alike every sort of opportunity to develop music's power to reveal the emotion and content within them. I am still convinced that this was Monteverdi's purpose and that, no matter how it is revealed, commitment of this sort must be our first concern in performing his music to twentieth-century audiences. A pallid, cautiously virginal approach does it less than justice.

In 1960 at the Royal Festival Hall I conducted a concert consisting of the first two acts of *L'Orfeo* and, in the second half, selected scenes from *L'incoronazione di Poppea*. Moran Caplat was aware of my enthusiasm for Monteverdi and attended with George Christie and various other Glyndebourne colleagues.

Be that as it may, the direct outcome was an invitation to prepare a version of the opera for Glyndebourne in 1962. Günther Rennert was to direct and Hugh Casson to create the sets. The costumes were created by Conwy Evans who produced some remarkable designs combining style, colour and dramatic purpose to great effect.

Initially it was the series of encounters with Rennert that proved of most value. I greatly admired his sort of theatrical imagination and also liked him very much. He was a 'paring-down' director and, although I had had a lot of experience in the theatre in Cambridge and in my first professional years, I was, of course, nothing like as experienced or as theatrically certain as he was. His sense of pace and structure stiffened my understanding of the piece and, therefore, the musical realisation of it in terms of performing it at Glyndebourne in 1962.

It must be explained here that Italian opera written between 1600 and 1670 needs considerable attention before it can be performed, due to the way it was conceived, written down and performed at that time. All we have left, for the most part, is a vocal line and a simple bass line. The lack of a 'full-score' kept these works on library shelves for three hundred years until the mists surrounding the Valhalla of the unquestionable, unadaptable *Urtext* were wafted aside and other ways of conceiving and performing opera were revealed. Suffice it to say that an opera from these earlier times in Italy has now to be reconstructed from the skeletal outlines and that my reconstruction was greatly influenced by those meetings with Rennert.

The question was then raised whether I would conduct or play in the performances and, since John Pritchard was keen about the piece, I agreed that it was better that he should conduct and I play the first harpsichord. At that time nobody had worked out how to direct successfully the recitative-music that accounted for about half the opera and was to be accompanied, as in Monteverdi's day, by a large group of free-playing instruments – organs, harp, lutes, chittarones and harpsichords. Their co-ordination with the stage within the limits of twentieth-century rehearsal conditions gave many problems which the normal skills of beating time would not resolve. The memories of that distinguished harpist, Maria Korchinska, who was quite unused to this uncountable music, in frenzied and totally committed lunges at her instrument in order to keep with John or a singer, will remain with me for ever. I sat immediately behind her in the pit. She loved the music and the part I had written had no technical worries for her. It was the controlled freedom of it all that caused the agitation. She wore her hair in a roll around her head and, by the end of each performance, she looked like some handsome Kentucky farmer's wife after a long day plucking turkeys; hair everywhere, but shining with a glow of achievement. Eventually she gave me a beautiful silver box she had brought with her from Russia because she had enjoyed the performances so much.

J.P. was, I think, never very comfortable with the recitative music and, in the last revival, somewhat happily handed the direction to me and, being a demon for punishment, I continued to play first harpsichord as well.

We were extremely fortunate in our cast and Glyndebourne was the ideal place for such a project without precedent. No one really knew how the piece would turn out.

Richard Lewis and Magda Laszlo as Nero and Poppea combined intuition and intelligence with superb musicianship. Rennert used wonderfully the experienced, somewhat contained sensuality of his Poppea to oppose the inner tensions that Richard Lewis's Welsh reserve brought to the part of Nero. They barely touched each other on stage and yet the sense that, in the distance of parting, there was growing an almost intolerable intensity proved immensely effective, even overpowering in the irony of the final scene where, amid the public splendour of Poppea's coronation they stood closest, unable to embrace. Carlo Cava as Seneca was unforgettably impressive and was himself amazingly moved. At the end of the last performance this huge, strong man was found back-stage weeping, inconsolable that he would not inhabit that part again at Glyndebourne. Oralia Dominguez sang Arnalta, Poppea's nurse, the only wholly likeable character in the opera. She sang the famous lullaby as wonderfully as one could ever hope for and the earthy, peasant-like care she showed for her charge, her wiliness and vanity in the last solo scene came to her and us as a wonderful gift of characterisation. Drusilla and Ottone, more simply realised as characters, were perfectly manifested in Lydia Marimpietri and Walter Alberti. Ottavia, a solitary, tragic figure, was beautifully understood and sung by Frances Bible; the two servants by Soo-Bee Lee and Duncan Robertson and, not least, Lucano, Nero's companion in corruption, was sung by Hugues Cuénod. I dare not say what monstrous object Harry Kellard, the propmaker, put instead of a stamen into the exotic flower that Hugues carried during his drunken orgy with Nero. It appeared, evidently, for the first time only on the first night and nearly made Hugues forget his lines. So experienced a horticulturalist, however, was not so easily defeated.

Throughout the rehearsals of this then unknown piece there grew an extraordinary sense of excitement. It occurs always during the best of Glyndebourne's projects. No one talks about it much. Theatre people are very superstitious and it might easily go away, but, once recognised, everyone nurtures it, in this case to great effect, for the opening of *Poppea* was an extraordinary evening even in that extraordinary place and the opera was repeated for three years running, something unknown in Glyndebourne's more recent history.

Still more important, as we can see in retrospect, a new vein had been found. Perhaps it was the shock of success, but at first the potential wasn't recognised and it didn't seem possible to follow it up.

In 1965 there was nothing. In 1966, Purcell's *Dido and Aeneas* made half a programme with Ravel's *L'Heure espagnole*, and Handel's *Jephtha* was given an evening to itself. Neither did very much to further matters. No great revelation was made by the *Dido* in spite of superb singing by Janet Baker, Sheila Armstrong and Patricia Johnson. The work was already well-known and Franco Enriquez was to do many more interesting productions for the company.

Jephtha must, equally, be considered as something of an unsuccessful by-blow. The oratorio was presented in a singularly static fashion, cruelly chopped about musically and, whatever it did for Hamburg (where it originated) in the way of revealing Handel's genius, it did very little in that way for English audiences. The score seemed to have been prepared by someone who supported the view that Handel was not only a theatrical dolt but also a man who could neither understand nor respond to the words he was setting: an odd verdict on someone who spent most of his highly successful life in the theatre. As in *Dido* the cast was unexceptionable with Heather Harper, Patricia Johnson, Margaret Price and Richard Lewis, but Rennert misconceived the piece, Caspar Neher followed suit and Leopold Ludwig's conducting was stolid and dull.

In 1967 Cavalli's *L'Ormindo* represented a return to the freer theatrical airs of *Poppea* and the journey of exploration into early Italian opera was moving forward again.

After *Poppea* I had spent some long time in Venice hoping to discover one of the lost Monteverdi operas. Instead, I discovered the extraordinary lyric talent of Francesco Cavalli. He is to Monteverdi, who taught him, what Schubert was to Beethoven. There was in the Marciana library a large collection of his operas, all in the same skeletal state as *Poppea*, waiting for a process of revivification. Flushed with my discovery of this wonderful and virtually unknown theatrical talent, I proposed *L'Ormindo* to Glyndebourne. They accepted and plans went forward. Rennert once more directed and responded brilliantly to the humour and wit of the piece as well as to the gradual darkening of the plot as it progresses to its near-tragic end. His desire to avoid the conventional led him to propose Erich Kondrak as designer, and some rather strange representations of the Moroccan desert came out of it. Without having much to do with the idea of seventeenth-century Venetian opera they served pretty well.

The cast was superb. The two main male protagonists were sung by Peter-Christoph Runge and John Wakefield, the latter one of the most striking and wonderfully gifted young tenors to appear in England at that time. It was a major tragedy for English music when the voice was irrevocably damaged and he abandoned singing. Peter-Christoph, happily, is still with us and occasionally returns to Glyndebourne. They were a wonderful pair, rivals for the love of the young queen Erisbe, initially miscast but changed during rehearsals and given to the young Anne Howells who rose to the challenge and had her first major success in that part. Jane Berbié as the Queen's maid, Isabel Garcisanz as the page, Nerillo, used their solo scenes (a feature of early Venetian opera) to the greatest effect. It must be told that on the first night Jane, who had no reason at all to be nervous, panicked and had literally to be pushed on the fore-stage after the third unrehearsed repetition of the opening *ritornello* to one of her scenes. In the pit (I was conducting) I couldn't imagine what had happened except that there were distinct flurries off-stage on the prompt side and no Jane on-stage. Once there, however, she brought the house down with her exposition of what lively young wives of impotent grey-beards should do with their time. The jealous, tormented King was played by Federico Davià who looked so magnificent and sang in such a way that the King's impotence became a tragic burden instead of something ridiculous. Irmgard Stadler was the mysterious Sicle out to regain the love of her former suitor, aided and abetted by Maureen Lehane and Hugues Cuénod in drag, another characteristic of early Venetian opera. It would seem that the singing of somewhat crotchety but wise and funny old women by men enabled them, as with our pantomime Dames, to say things that would otherwise be unacceptable. Hugues was incredibly funny but it was all done within the bounds of good taste, probably, like George Robey, the funnier for that. The pathos of Sicle apart, the trio, Stadler, Lehane and Cuénod conspiring about the stage was unforgettable.

The response of Glyndebourne audiences confirmed that we were on the right track again and *L'Ormindo* was repeated with equal success in 1968. We even took it to the Cuvilliès theatre in Munich when the Glyndebourne company was invited there in 1969. It takes a long time to prepare one of these early Venetian operas for performance, and, although wheels were in motion and the realisation begun, there was a gap in 1969 before a second Cavalli piece could be fully prepared. This time, in 1970, it was *La Calisto*, a version of Ovid's Metamorphic story of how the little bear (Ursa minor) came to shine in the night sky. The director was to be Peter Hall whom I had known and worked with in London and

44

9 and 10   The British-Italian connection. Sesto Bruscantini and Ian
  Wallace in *La cenerentola* (1952) and (*right*) Graziella Sciutti and
  Geraint Evans in *Figaro* (1958)

11   The 1954 *Barbiere di Siviglia*: Wallace, Oncina, Cassinelli,
  Sciutti and Bruscantini

12, 13 and 14   Some figures of the mid-1950s: *above left*, Teresa
Berganza as Cherubino; *above right*, Vittorio Gui in rehearsal;
below, *Figaro*, Act IV, in Oliver Messel's set

15, 16 and 17   The late 1950s: *above left*, Günther Rennert
directing; *above right*, Régine Crespin makes her British début
as the Marschallin in *Der Rosenkavalier*; *below*, Glyndebourne's
first production of *The Rake's Progress* goes under the television
cameras

18 Jani Strasser, Glyndebourne's long-serving and highly
demanding Chief Repetiteur, coaches Carlo Cava in *Il barbiere
di Siviglia* (1961)

19 Luciano Pavarotti makes his only Glyndebourne appearance, as
Idamante in *Idomeneo*, with Gundula Janowitz as Ilia and
Richard Lewis as Idomeneo (1964)

Stratford since Cambridge days, and the designer was to
be John Bury whom I did not know. It proved to be a
wonderfully stimulating collaboration with much early
concentration given to the problems of translating seventeenth-century Venetian opera on to the twentieth-
century stage. It was not just a matter of re-working the
idea of machines that would transport the gods from
Parnassus to Earth, but also how that resulting immediate and rapid interaction of gods and humans could be
made to expose emotions and intentions that would
illuminate lively ideas and conditions for us mortals
sitting in the stalls at Glyndebourne.

It was, for the three of us, a matter of posing,
discussing and resolving questions in the same way, each
at once respecting and stimulating the other. Except
with *Il ritorno d'Ulisse* where the same company deliber-
ated and resolved still graver problems, I have never felt
more fulfilled in the theatre.

The plot of *La Calisto* is concerned with the attempts
of Jove (Ugo Trama) to seduce Calisto (Ileana Cotrubas),
one of the nymphs of the virgin goddess, Diana (Janet
Baker). She, more concerned with her mistress than
anything else, repulses his first advances until, at the
instigation of Mercury (Peter Gottlieb), Jove disguises
himself as Diana and is enchanted to find Calisto
remarkably responsive. The confusion that results with
the real Diana may be imagined. She, in her turn, is
loved by Pan (Federico Davià). And Diana, surrounded
by her nymphs (including an elderly, crotchety but
sexually curious Linfea, played, once more in drag, by
Hugues Cuénod), casts longing, amorous glances on
Endymion (James Bowman). Juno (Irmgard Stadler),
with the chill of cold reality on her lips, descends with
her peacocks to put matters to right and change Calisto
into a sylvan Ursa minor.

All is sexual ambiguity and, the comedy of the

situations apart, quite serious questions are posed by the piece which were truthfully and brilliantly expounded in Peter Hall's direction. The basic design by John Bury was a long A shape that seemed to stretch from here to Olympus. Forests appeared and vanished in a moment, a fountain sprang water and suddenly was no more. In a whirl of a gorgeous feathered cloak the little bear became Calisto again, transformed through Jove's compassion or conscience, depending on your view of the situation.

In Cavalli's original manuscript at the moment when Jove transforms himself into the image of his daughter, Diana, the music changes from the bass clef to the treble. This gave rise to the attractive idea that Jove should sing falsetto when playing Diana. It was further encouraged by the knowledge that Ugo Trama, always a strong candidate for the part, warmed up his voice an octave or so above its normal tessitura. He bravely agreed to play the double role and we began rehearsals. Every time we came to a Jove-as-Diana scene a general air of hilarity set in which, as it grew, put Peter and myself into deeper and deeper gloom. Funny the piece was, camp and silly it was not. After, perhaps, six days we had a run-through and asked various people so far not connected with the production to come and listen. Danny la Rue would have been delighted at the reception. You could hardly hear the piece for laughter but it was all about one joke and nothing to do with the subtle, intricate opera we were trying to put on. The rehearsal ended and everyone concerned with the production went his own way without even discussing it. At some unearthly hour next morning Peter and I spoke on the telephone and agreed to meet right away in the conductor's room at Glyndebourne. We had both come to the same conclusion: it was Diana who must play the double part of herself and Jove transformed into her own

image. After a breakfast consultation with the management we telephoned Janet Baker who had retreated to
her home in London for the night and put the proposal to
her. Practical as ever, she asked for half an hour to look
at the score and think about it, after which she telephoned back to say she would do it. Ugo Trama, whose
part was cut more or less in half, behaved better than
most would have done and agreed to the change. Janet
had taken on a singing and acting challenge which, as it
turned out, gave her one of the most memorable parts of
her career, and a challenge to which she rose with
genius. In the same costume with only a staff to
symbolise the difference, she played both parts, the
lascivious Jove and the virginal Diana beset by her own
love for Endymion, with such skill that there was never a
moment's doubt for the audience as to who was on stage
even when one followed the other within seconds. She
was alternately funny and lecherous, then touching and
vulnerable.

La Calisto amused, moved, entertained and even
educated the more discerning Glyndebourne audiences
for three seasons. It was revived in 1971 and 1974. I used
to think sometimes at performances how much old John
Christie would have enjoyed it. He might even have
wanted to play Sylvano, the earthy woodland creature;
after all his granddaughter played the bear.

In between the last two revivals the latest and, until
now, the last of the Venetian line, Monteverdi's *Il ritorno
d'Ulisse*, was produced in 1972. For some years doubts
had been cast upon the authenticity of this, the last of
the great man's operas. The gravity of its music, in
fitting contrast to the overt sensuality of *Poppea* and the
lack of an autograph had left the decision with those who
squabbled about it without any certain knowledge or
ability to perceive its quality. The work only needed to
be imagined creatively and as a piece of musical theatre

for it to be revealed as an overpowering operatic masterpiece, showing an understanding and response to the human condition comparable only to classical drama or Shakespeare.

During its preparation the sense of excitement at working on so great a piece grew and endured through one complete version of the opera and then another after my house burned down, destroying the entire first manuscript. There were formidable technical and dramatic problems which the three of us, Peter Hall, John Bury and I, discussed and pondered. At least there was an aesthetic for tackling this style of opera already prepared for by *La Calisto*, but the much grander scale of *Ulisse* and the scope of its drama meant that everything had to be re-thought. We had to give the sense of two approaching destinies, one, personified by Ulysses, returning at last from Troy, and the other by Penelope waiting still on Ithaca beset by terrible and increasing dangers, each of them surveyed by the gods, themselves divided into two warring factions. The gods as gods (Minerva, Ulysses' especial protector, becomes at one point a shepherd boy and descends to Ithaca) must stay in the skies and be able to move about. Neptune must rise up there from the seas to play his part in the dispute, the Phoenicians, who help Ulysses to Ithaca, must be transformed, with their departing ship, into a rock and, worst of all, Ulysses must shoot the suitors with his great bow in a scene of carnage that must convince us as well as provide a fitting theatrical climax to the opera. The final solution for this last, of using real arrows which thudded into wooden tables and flew into the wings, shot from a real bow drawn by Ulysses, initially caused some alarm. But so skilfully was it staged that it was all perfectly safe and yet gave an unforgettable image of revengeful destruction with Penelope (Janet Baker) standing in the midst of it all, quite unharmed, while

Minerva, above, guided and protected her beloved Ulysses (Benjamin Luxon).

Technical and scenic matters apart, the hardest question was how to show Penelope, after waiting twenty years for Ulysses to return from Troy, prepared to reject him by refusing recognition even after the holocaust. Peter's great gift for asking the right theatrical questions provided the most wonderful answer. Like a war-widow who has become accustomed to her situation and is suddenly confronted by her lost husband, she would not, could not face the reality of it, for in those years she had nearly become somebody else. So Ulysses, the wily fox who survived Troy and understands, has to woo her all over again. Somehow this last courtship and the final hymn-like duet celebrating love recovered after so long, became one of the greatest moments many of us had experienced in the theatre. At the end of the first night Ben Luxon broke down and on the last night so did Janet. On most nights most of us were pretty close to it.

The rest of the cast was superb with Anne Howells a resplendent Minerva, Richard Lewis a vigorously benign Eumete, Virginia Popova as Penelope's wise old nurse, Clifford Grant as Neptune. The three villainous suitors were played by Bernard Dickerson, John Fryatt and Ugo Trama, Iro, the glutton, by Alexander Oliver and the smaller roles were admirably done by members of the company. Each performance was something of an occasion, like setting out on a long, arduous and important journey.

Ulisse was repeated in 1973 and then again in 1979, in the latter year with Frederica von Stade and Richard Stilwell as Penelope and Ulysses. Ann Murray replaced Anne Howells with equal flair and virtuosity. With this last cast the opera was recorded for CBS.

After that the well of seventeenth-century opera has, for the time being, dried up. Monteverdi is now widely performed and in many differing versions. Cavalli, too, has become a known, accepted composer. His two operas which saw the light of twentieth-century day at Glyndebourne have been played in many other houses and I have realised two more, *L'Egisto* and *L'Orione* which after appearing first at Santa Fe, have been widely performed. Several other of his operas have now been revived in America and Europe. As with Rossini, Glyndebourne's influence has been seminal.

In the most recent years, however, earlier opera has not featured in the season's programmes. Perhaps it is a case of *reculer pour mieux sauter* and in due course a different seam, maybe of Handel or Rameau, will be explored and found to be full of silver, or should it be gold? At any rate it will be particular.

Glyndebourne & Rossini

The Stylistic Approach

John Pritchard

The first bar of Rossini's overture to *Il barbiere di Siviglia* (which was annexed from his *Elisabetta, regina d'Inghilterra*) begins with a favourite device of the composer: a forceful and imperative attack on the chord of E major, rather resembling a 'rat-tat' on some closed and impressive portal,. which must open to reveal various delights. Of course Rossini was following contemporary practice in assuming that a loud summons, or perhaps several, would be necessary if the evening's proceedings were to get under way, with the fashionable Rome

51

audience at last persuaded to abate their conversation and settle into their seats. I often think the realistic composer may have delighted in the implied reproach to that restive audience, evidenced by the springy *pianissimo* which follows the first loud orchestral bang: almost certainly the buzz of talk persisted until a moment later a second emphatic summons assailed the ears, the soft little scurrying figure ensuing – as though Rossini said, 'Why not listen to it the first time?'

Curiously enough, discussion of this 'rat-tat' in the *Barbiere* overture plunges Rossini conductors straight into a practical and stylistic difficulty which, in a small way, encapsulates questions of much more far-reaching implication in the performance of his operas. Since every craftsman's professional approach to his job is usually of some interest, a brief consideration of this musical 'motto' is not irrelevant to our subject; because the attitude of Glyndebourne from the very beginning of its Rossini series was in effect to say unequivocally – 'Rossini is *not* Mozart. His music, though perhaps in texture similar, derives from a totally different creative impulse in which, perhaps for the first time in musical history, wit touched with irony is given a very clear form. Thus the music of Rossini – at Glyndebourne – is to be performed and translated into stage action with emphasis on its intrinsic *wit*, which in turn must imply refinement of treatment.' Of course Glyndebourne would never be didactic enough to express the matter thus, but in effect the ideology behind the entire Rossini series could have been summarised in some such way.

When I was a young conductor, performing in concert the overture of *Barbiere*, I used to worry about the technique of getting the first 'rat-tat' chords *together*: nervous wavings in the empty air, giving the already apprehensive musicians silent beats, produced (eight times out of ten) a minor rhythmic shambles. The public, expecting to enjoy a trouble-free experience of favourite music, were understandably irritated when the very beginning of the programme displayed the orchestra in disarray, and were inclined to be censorious of the musical inexperience of the conductor, who had as it were 'shuffled' his way into the Overture.

Some years later, when I was Vittorio Gui's disciple and assistant in the Glyndebourne 'Rossini team', I of course questioned the Maestro about this vexing little problem arising throughout the Rossini overtures and the operas themselves. Vittorio, laconic in oracle-like utterance, replied in a sentence which I have never forgotten and which for me resolved the question totally: 'Pa-pa', he said, 'is pa-pa!' At once I sensed, more than in the answer to a probably needless question, a whole attitude of practicality and instinctive understanding of Rossini's intentions; for Gui had no objection to shortening Rossini's *written* notes in these instances to fulfil the composer's practical aim – to arrest attention. However, in a somewhat similarly assertive beginning in Mozart's *Zauberflöte* Overture

a conductor would never dream of playing anything other than the exact printed rhythm. The reason is that with Mozart we are in a world of musical symbolism, based on the composer's use throughout the opera of the 'Three-Chord' motif associated with Masonry, and no abbreviation here would be appropriate or possible. I have often thought that if one could accept as a definition of *style* 'an informed and *instinctive* interpretation of the composer's intentions in comparison with or contrast to his contemporaries', then Rossini has to be approached not merely with the respect due to a lucky (albeit meteoric) musical inventor, but as a composer bringing unique insight into the realm of *opera buffa*.

It was this belief in the particular role of Rossini which from his early years had activated Vittorio Gui and was to bring him to a position as surely the most authoritative interpreter of the operas in this century: Glyndebourne can never congratulate itself enough on the almost haphazard chain of events which engaged Gui for nine successive seasons beginning in 1952, in which he, together with Carl Ebert as stage director and Oliver Messel as designer, established a level of Rossini performance which remains a model – alas, I fear, a model still to be fully studied or emulated elsewhere in the operatic firmament. My own experience around the world in many opera houses (and as Music Director in three of them) is that a new production of a Rossini opera, instead of being a mirror of the grace, style and glitter of the music, is too often an excuse for yet another banal romp and exaggerated scenic farce, which it is mistakenly thought the opera requires if it is to 'bring the house down'.

When with Gui as a kindly but exigent supervisor we addressed ourselves at Glyndebourne to the preparation of the first Rossini production in the Sussex theatre (*Cenerentola* in 1952), I think the choice of an opera less familiar than *Barbiere* was dictated by Gui's love for the work; but it was selected also because he rightly thought it would take a little time and experience for Rossini's most popular opera, victim of many jolly rollicking performances in England and Europe generally, to be sufficiently laundered and purified to be presented in an authentic and stylistic staging at Glyndebourne. In fact, we had to wait another two years until the Gui-Ebert-Messel trio turned out an impeccable *Barbiere*. This production, for me and a generation to whom this opera was on the whole a joy liberally laced with embarrassment, at last showed the comic masterpiece in its pristine colours.

First, however, in the series we had *Cenerentola*, which the British public were willing to forgive for not *quite* following their own beloved fairy-story, and at once were guided by Gui into realising the crucial importance of judicious casting of the main roles – an approach to casting moreover somewhat different from that used for the Mozart operas, in which Glyndebourne was so experienced. Spike Hughes, in one of the Glyndebourne programme articles, has referred to the 'Gui Male Voice Trio' which formed the centrepiece of *Cenerentola*, *Barbiere* and *Comte Ory*. The redoubtable Juan Oncina, Sesto Bruscantini and Ian Wallace indeed adorned these particular productions with a consortium of talents: Oncina, a mellifluous and fluent tenor with the essential high notes employed with a roguish eye; Bruscantini, the master of stage timing, combined with complete vocal flexibility; and Wallace, not born to Italianate utterance, but quick, instinctive and commendably unexaggerated in *buffo* roles. For his female *protagonista* Gui selected the Spanish mezzo, Marina de Gabarain, and accepted her occasional waywardness of rhythm for the sake of the typically Spanish soft-grained vocal quality, which later Teresa Berganza displayed, of course, to perfection.

It is, looking back, no exaggeration to say that to begin the study of a Rossini opera score was from the very start a re-education in Gui's hands. His belief and acceptance as self-evident that the Italian melodic phrase – perfected in his other love, Bellini – stood calm and enduring above the buffets of musical fashion, was endearing and somehow led musicians and singers into tranquil accord, so that an ensemble or big concerted finale presented few surprises or pitfalls. It was not necessary (I realised as I accompanied so many musical rehearsals at the piano) to keep a wary eye on the Maestro to accommodate some quirk of 'interpretation'. With Gui all would be reasonable, satisfying and – to employ a strange word applied to musical performance – 'wholesome': as a young conductor I would, like all young conductors, occasionally think 'why doesn't he get a move on?' – only to realise in a moment, as Rossini's vocal melisma and cascades of runs ensued, how wise and practical a steady tempo had been from the outset. Only when there was a lapse of taste, an ungracious high note held too long or a breathy*staccato* instead of a *legato* phrase, would Gui intervene: 'No, no ... meglio così.' His method was really to find singers he could trust, show them how he wanted the music to be performed, and set the machine in agreeable operation. There were indeed few disagreements in those early musical ensemble rehearsals.

At times the temptation to have a little innocent fun at the expense of this immensely cultured but endlessly loquacious Maestro was irresistible. I remember one day, in the hall of the Christies' house, as Gui was descending the stairs from his room, I slipped Giulini's recording of the *Cenerentola* overture on to the gramophone. Vittorio immediately asked who was conducting and listened calmly: suddenly the strings could be heard playing *pizzicato* instead of with the bow, as Gui considered correct. To him, an error of taste or scholarship perpetrated by a fellow-Italian was doubly heinous, and I was rewarded with a lengthy discourse on the Rossini manuscripts, Gui's lifelong familiarity with them, and what seemed to me (itching to escape into the sunshine) a verbal town-plan of the city of Pesaro, where Gui had studied the original Rossini scores.

This leads me to a brief mention of the Rossini orchestral material – an important factor in the musical texture of performance, but one which has led many theatres nowadays eagerly to adopt an almost irresistibly scholarly edition prepared by a noted Italian conductor. Vittorio Gui mistrusted any such general solution to the problems of *Urtext* in Rossini: he was a combative scholar himself and dearly loved a scuffle with the Italian Establishment as represented, say, by La Scala, Milan or the most famous music publishers. One must guard against the possibility of a certain injured vanity influencing the situation, in that Gui had not been consulted about the new edition, which as a revered expert in the field he might have expected. Nevertheless, when it came to *Barbiere*, Gui trusted the edition prepared from the autograph in the Conservatoire at Bologna, while the Overture was copied from the autograph in the Rossini Institute at Pesaro, where the composer was born. I must say that in my turn I have relied on this edition whenever I have conducted *Barbiere* in the USA or Europe, and found it a satisfying mirror in every respect of what a Rossinian could *believe* the composer to have penned. When musicologists have had their exhaustive say (as I have found in another field with the scores of Haydn) there is still a considerable 'grey area' in which the experience and instinct of the performer are called in play to arrive at a decision. Luckily these textual matters, though important to the interpreters themselves, rarely affect the enjoyment of listeners to any great extent (unless, for instance, the conductor persists in employing three modern trombones in the Overture of *Barbiere*!).

What we learnt, then, from over ten years' experience in casting the Rossini comedies was that a gallery of performers with special talents, exemplified by the Male Trio I have mentioned, became a *sine qua non*:

  – a *mezzo-soprano* with vocal agility and charm (*Barbiere, Cenerentola, Italiana*)

  – a *tenore leggiero*, with easy access to high notes and with vivid stage personality (*Barbiere, Ory, Turco, Cenerentola*)

  – a *basso buffo* with great agility in fast music and impeccable stage timing (*Barbiere, Cenerentola*)

  – a brilliant baritone, usually in the role of manipulator of the action (*Barbiere, Cenerentola, Ory*)

  – a true *basso cantante* with rich low notes and sense of comedy, an unusual combination (*Barbiere, Italiana, Turco*).

The list, which is incomplete, reveals at a glance the problems facing operatic managements today. It is strange how various countries and regions of the world, in a changing pattern, have contributed gifted performers to this essential gallery. Thus for a time the especially Latin talents of Supervia, Simionato, de Gabarain, Berganza facilitated the casting of the leading female roles; Valetti, Alva, Oncina, Benelli, Gedda for the tenors; Stabile, Bruscantini, Corena, Montarsolo, Carlos Feller, in a splending gallery of *bassi buffi*; Gobbi, Panerai, Bruscantini for the brilliant baritones; Baccaloni, Tajo, Siepi, Rossi-Lemeni, Carlo Cava the *bassi cantanti*. The sopranos, for once relegated to last mention on our roster, of course produced Graziella Sciutti, Alda Noni – and (to drop a name) Maria Callas.

Practically all of these performers had or have a lively sense of comedy, and most of them came under the kindly discipline of Vittorio Gui, many actually at

Glyndebourne or in performance in Italian theatres. It would be quite instructive today to try to compile a comparable list of currently active 'Rossini artists', and to examine how far the adoption of a purified performance style in the operas has spread beyond the Italian shores (including, for this purpose, Glyndebourne as an Italian protectorate!). Even if we are fearful of overlooking the claims of some good Rossini artists not mentioned, we could cite among the mezzo-sopranos Marilyn Horne, Frederica von Stade (USA), Ann Murray (Irish Republic), Alicia Nafé (Argentina); considering the tenors produces the name of Francisco Araiza (Mexico), followed by an embarrassing pause – with a hopeful look towards promising newcomers such as Rockwell Blake and John Aler (USA); with the *bassi buffi*, one must hasten on, grateful only that the stalwart Carlos Feller (Argentina) and Bruscantini still give object lessons in such roles as Bartolo and Don Magnifico; baritones are a shade easier, with the skills of Hermann Prey, Wolfgang Brendel (West Germany), Berndt Weikl (Austria), Ingmar Wixell (Sweden) and Leo Nucci (Italy); for the basses, apart from a respectful look towards Giorgio Tozzi (USA) and Justino Diaz (Puerto Rico), I must ask for a recess until perhaps the Glyndebourne Centenary book in the year 2034 may indicate a more optimistic picture?

Rossini's operas still *do* get performed, extensively in the United Kingdom and USA and also (I am rather sorry to say) in Germany. My regret about Germany is occasioned by my impression – in which I should be delighted to find myself wrong – that hardly one of the lessons with which this essay is concerned has been learned there in the course of the last thirty years. In brief, this is because of the permanent addiction of Intendants to the idea that Rossini's place in the German opera repertoire is under the heading 'Spiel-Oper' (or a comedy with music): the artificiality of the plots is then rammed home with translation into German (as though the mostly fragile fiction needed ferociously trivial productions, decked out with painful visual gags. It is not too much to say that in only one of Germany's 200-odd opera houses – and that one I am far too modest to name – could an opera-goer be fairly confident of fulfilment from the stylistic viewpoint when visiting a Rossini performance.

However, lest it be thought that I am adopting too high-minded an attitude towards a country which devotes a huge national budget to the performance and maintenance of opera, I am reminded that some time ago, an important opera house in the United States, humouring one of its singers, allowed a vital recitative to be cut. This, of course, left a gaping hole in the plot and, the characters' subsequent behaviour was no longer logical. It is unfair to point an accusing finger at German distortion of Rossini, without saying that it can happen in other countries too.

The feeling that opera establishments care little, providing the box office receipts do not fall off, means that conductors and stage directors invited to direct Rossini opera performances must continually be on their guard. On the musical side we have a mainly good edition available and singers on the whole are as meticulous as their forerunners in accepting guidance on matters of accuracy and phrasing. It is in my opinion in the field of stage production that the menace threatens.

I hope my colleagues, the stage producers and designers, will allow me a final swipe in their direction. I have been deterred only by the specialist interest of the subject from writing to *The Times* demanding a Charter for Opera Conductors, and since some of its clauses apply with particular force to Rossini productions, I ask indulgence to outline them here for international guidance.

1 No, ABSOLUTELY NO, stage action or mime or symbolism during the Overture.
2 No scrim or gauze aimed at giving diffused lighting on the stage – it *does* affect the acoustics, and singers detest it.
3 No enlargement of the stage apron by erection of supporting structures in the orchestra pit; no steps into the orchestra utilised by the stage performers; no mounting of lighting equipment in the pit; nothing to fall into the orchestra pit!
4 A more positive acceptance of the validity of the great concerted ensemble as an intrinsic (and mainly static) ingredient of opera; perhaps, even, an encouragement to accept the set-pieces at face value, in need of no accompanying distracting stage movement either by swaying, rocking or marching (I have yet to see an audience whose attention is not riveted by the great operatic *concertato*).
5 More realisation of the fact that it is VOCAL excellence which in the last resort draws people into opera performances: therefore the available budget must be stretched in the direction of providing fine voices, wherever they can be found, rather than in the building of expensive sets and needlessly rich costumes. One producer not long ago in Brussels asked for 2,600 'props' and when refused went on to Geneva to demand 3,400 in *Traviata*, including fake ash in the ash-trays!
6 The provision in rehearsal plans of *regular* musical ensemble rehearsals, *interrupting* the sequence of staging rehearsals so that the musical levels are maintained. Stage directors must be barred from these rehearsals.

POSTSCRIPT

A stage director friend to whom I showed this charter was piqued and countered with: 'First and foremost, the conductor shall maintain the *same* tempi in rehearsals and performances, and not cover the singers by the loud orchestra.'

Other Operas

Desmond Shawe-Taylor

When I was asked to write about 'Other Operas', I did not feel that I had been allotted the leftovers from more solid categories of fare. Far from it. I instantly recalled that the very first steps taken by Glyndebourne outside the charmed circle of Mozart, just before the war, had provided me with one altogether delightful experience, and another which I count to this day among the most memorable and formative experiences of my operatic life.

This was Verdi's *Macbeth*, first seen in 1938. Although the Verdi revival had been under way in Germany for some years, *Macbeth* was at that time a totally unknown work to all but a few specialists in England. Its arrival was due to Fritz Busch's intense love of Verdi, and his previous association with Carl Ebert and the designer, Caspar Neher, in several Verdi projects in Germany. What this theatrical trinity displayed to our dazzled eyes and ears on that distant May evening was nothing short of a revelation.

In a sense, the Mozart operas of the preceding years

63

had been that too; but then the operatic genius of Mozart was undisputed, and there was moreover one flaw in those fine productions – the undistinguished sets and costumes. In *Macbeth* everything came together: the bracing shock of the unknown masterpiece, the unifying force of conducting, production and stage picture, and superb portrayals of the leading roles. This last element was still more marked in the 1939 revival, when Vera Schwarz (herself a much stronger artist than I should have suspected from various performances seen at the Vienna State Opera) was replaced in the role of Lady Macbeth by the unknown, but vocally and dramatically magnificent, Margherita Grandi. 'Tasmanian', said the programme, mysteriously; and there always remained something mysterious about this soprano, apparently a pupil of Calvé, who reappeared after the war, in somewhat diminished voice, and whose later life has proved difficult to trace. Fine as it was, the Sleepwalking Scene that she recorded for HMV with Beecham in 1948 was nothing like the electrifying performance she used to give with Busch in 1939.

The second extra-Mozartian step was the *Don Pasquale* of Donizetti; and that too made us feel that there was rather more to Italian opera than we had realised at Covent Garden. Audrey Mildmay, playing the pretended spitfire somewhat against the grain of her genial temperament, was the Norina, and Dino Borgioli the graceful Ernesto; but what really made these performances was the rare combination of the scheming Dr Malatesta of Mariano Stabile, characteristically leaning back to relish every turn in the discomfiture of his victim, and the victim himself, in the delightfully rotund person of Salvatore Baccaloni.

These two works combined to form a glorious beginning to non-Mozartian activities at Glyndebourne; but then came the war, during which only a touring *Beggar's*

Opera, directed by John Gielgud, could be managed, with Michael Redgrave as Macheath and Audrey Mildmay as Polly. In 1946 came the more momentous première of Britten's *The Rape of Lucretia*, again followed by many performances on tour; but neither of these could quite qualify as Glyndebourne productions. Gluck's *Orfeo* in 1947 was a move back towards normality, and the work itself was certainly a natural choice for Glyndebourne. It was a worthy attempt, although Kathleen Ferrier, the dignified heroine, was then still a beginner in the field of opera, and unsure of her Italian, while Fritz Stiedry's conducting was sadly insensitive. Not until thirty-five years later, on the occasion of Janet Baker's farewell to the stage, was substantial justice done at Glyndebourne to Gluck's masterpiece. In the intervening period, there had been several bites at the same composer's *Alceste*, but no attempt was made to tackle *Armide* or either of the two *Iphigenie*s, which struck many musicians as no less appropriate to the house.

For the rest, those early post-war years consisted to a considerable extent of productions mounted by Glyndebourne for the Edinburgh Festival. This was administered by Rudolf Bing, who in 1947 was both general manager of Glyndebourne and artistic director of the Edinburgh Festival, before in 1948 he left to devote all his time to Edinburgh. Inevitably they were geared in the first place to the frustrating inadequacies of the King's Theatre of that city. Here, apart from Mozart and Strauss, Verdi was the principal attraction, with a somewhat less glorious revival of the pre-war *Macbeth* and new productions of *La forza del destino* and *Un ballo in maschera* (the latter rather opulently alternating Margherita Grandi and Ljuba Welitsch as Amelia: I remember thinking that they resembled the White Queen and the Red Queen respectively, the one inclined to be a bit vague, the other decisive and apt to cry 'Faster! faster!').

There was also in Edinburgh in 1955 a Giulini/Ebert Glyndebourne *Falstaff*, precursor of several subsequent and coarser performances of this *echt*-Glyndebourne opera; and in 1960, the last Edinburgh season in which Glyndebourne participated, a production of Bellini's *I Puritani*, with Joan Sutherland as the heroine, which had been seen earlier that summer in Sussex. In the same year, a triple bill was offered of Wolf-Ferrari's *Il segreto di Susanna*, Poulenc's *La Voix humaine* (with Denise Duval as the splendid original interpreter of this Cocteau monologue) and Busoni's *Arlecchino*: all three of which either had been, or would be, seen at Glyndebourne in different couplings. More significant than these was the British première of Stravinsky's *The Rake's Progress* in 1953. This work was in later years to be repeatedly revived at Glyndebourne, where it proved the one completely successful modern opera until the happy arrival of Britten's *Midsummer Night's Dream* in 1981.

It was during the early 1950s that Glyndebourne became fully itself again; perhaps the turning point (although outside the scope of this chapter) was the first English professional performance of Mozart's *Idomeneo* in 1951. In considering the work of the subsequent thirty years, in so far as it falls under my heading, I propose to divide the repertory, somewhat arbitrarily, into two groups of unequal size: in the first place, classical and nineteenth-century operas; in the second place, modern or recent operas. The border-line between the two, as between the nineteenth and twentieth centuries, is marked by Debussy's *Pelléas et Mélisande* – in many ways the perfect Glyndebourne opera.

The first of my two categories is by far the larger. Apart from the already-discussed Gluck, it begins in chronological order of composition, though by no means in chronological order of Glyndebourne presentation, with Haydn: his *La fedeltà premiata* of 1780, which came to Glyndebourne in 1979 and 1980. Haydn is an operatic problem; and it is clear that Glyndebourne has found him so. One of the greatest and most versatile of the classical composers, and moreover concerned for a great part of his active life, to a degree that has only lately been realised, with the composition and presentation of opera, he yet lacked some essential dramatic spark; and this lack distinguishes his operas painfully from those of Mozart, and even of far lesser composers such as Cimarosa and Donizetti, not to mention Rossini.

The flaw is partly temperamental, no doubt, and partly the consequence of his having lived his entire operatic life, not in some busy centre of the art such as Venice or Vienna, Milan or Naples, but in the magnificent provinciality of Esterház. (In our own time, I venture to suggest, Benjamin Britten achieved slightly less than he might have achieved in the field of opera, because of his obstinate preference for the Aldeburgh scale and conditions over those of the greater operatic world, which should have been his natural habitat, but which he increasingly disliked and distrusted.) Many Haydn scholars insist that he is a great opera composer rather than a great opera composer *manqué*; I am not convinced. That his operas contain much superb music is beyond question. At all events, the style of John Cox's production of *La fedeltà premiata* and of Sir Hugh Casson's designs (with suggestions of a show-within-a-show and arch allusions to the physical ambience of Glyndebourne itself) clearly betrayed a lack of confidence in the opera as a self-sufficient work of art. Yet at first sight Haydn's operas would seem ideal material for the extension of the Glyndebourne repertory; possibly the more serious works, *Armida* or *Orlando Paladino*, might stand a better chance of success there.

In 1965 Glyndebourne put on, with fair success, Cimarosa's *Il matrimonio segreto*, elegantly produced by

Frank Hauser, designed by Desmond Heeley and conducted in the first few performances by Myer Fredman
and subsequently by Gui. The fate of this opera is
curious. From having been what might be called 'the
rich man's *Figaro*' (a far greater hit in court circles than
Mozart's immortal comedy), it has become in our day
very much 'the poor man's *Figaro*': constantly recalling
Mozart's work of six years earlier in style and general lay-
out, but always disappointing us by its obviously inferior
invention and workmanship. The comedies of Rossini
and Donizetti are not the equal of Mozart, either; but
they have their own zest and their own manner of the
new century, so that they never seem like an inferior
imitation.

An opera that has undoubtedly proved itself at
Glyndebourne is *Fidelio*. Rather surprisingly, Ebert (as
Spike Hughes tells us in his history of Glyndebourne)
had always considered Beethoven's opera unsuitable to a
'Woods-and-Meadows Festival Programme'; but Busch
felt otherwise – although, by the time it appeared in the
programme, in 1959, Busch was dead, and *Fidelio* was
presented by the somewhat improbable combination of
Vittorio Gui as conductor and Günther Rennert as
producer, and with the admirable Gré Brouwenstijn as
the heroine. Twenty years later, the opera received a
new and even more notable revival, with Bernard
Haitink in the pit and Peter Hall as producer, and with
Elisabeth Söderström (later, Josephine Barstow) as
Leonore.

Donizetti, especially comic Donizetti, might seem
made for Glyndebourne; yet twenty-three years elapsed
between the already chronicled pre-war *Don Pasquale*
and the *Elisir d'amore* of 1961. Franco Zeffirelli, turning
for inspiration to old theatrical prints, made a delightful
thing out of the rustic comedy, especially of the elaborate and exuberant wedding-party set-piece that opens

the second act; although some of the singing was on the crude side, Luigi Alva's lovelorn Nemorino delighted the house, especially in the following year, when he had the young Mirella Freni as his Adina and Bruscantini as Dulcamara.

Four years after *L'elisir d'amore*, in 1965, Glyndebourne took the further step, which may have seemed bold then, of tackling a serious Donizetti opera: his *Anna Bolena*, to an excellent libretto by Romani. 'Give me a good book', the composer used to say, 'and I will give you a good opera'; and it was no idle boast. Consequently, although the cast had none of the brilliance of the famous 1957 revival of La Scala (under the same conductor, Gianandrea Gavazzeni), and the stage presentation by Franco Enriquez was mediocre, the opera had a considerable success, and was revived in 1968. All the same, no further investigation of either side of Donizetti's prolific genius has since been undertaken at Glyndebourne; and Bellini, too, has had no production since that *Puritani* of 1960.

It was rather to Russian and to French opera that the management next turned; and none too soon, since both these national schools were at that time much neglected in England. The first Glyndebourne venture into Russian opera was Tchaikovsky's *Eugene Onegin* in 1968, sensitively conducted by John Pritchard, produced by Michael Hadjimischev and designed by Pier Luigi Pizzi; with Elisabeth Söderström as an ideal Tatyana. Three years later, it was followed by *The Queen of Spades*, with the same conductor, producer and designer, but with a less interesting cast, apart from the old Countess of Virginia Popova (who had had the smaller part of the Nurse in *Onegin*). Less successful was Glyndebourne's attempt at a delicate Massenet style for *Werther*. Michael Redgrave's production and Henry Bardon's sets were unpretentiously appropriate; but the cast was frankly inadequate in 1966 – though somewhat improved in the 1969 revival.

Altogether superior – in fact, one of Glyndebourne's happiest achievements – was the *Pelléas et Mélisande* first seen there in 1962, and twice revived later in the decade, and again – with new and less appropriate décor – in 1976. Debussy's work, one of the few flawless things in the confused and dusty corridors of opera, seemed as though made for Glyndebourne: something which cannot quite hold its own in the rough and tumble of the big all-purpose opera house, but under favourable conditions can seem the loveliest music in the world. Glyndebourne, dedicated to the cult of perfection, is a natural home for this tender plant – even though the *buffo*-conditioned patrons of the house hardly knew, at first, how to take it, and were inclined to whisper through the marvellous orchestral interludes. The performance, if not ideal, was highly distinguished and often very moving.

Vittorio Gui, whose association with *Pelléas* dated back to Debussy's lifetime, drew from the Royal Philharmonic Orchestra an account of the score that was transparent and fresh in colour, and incisive in accent too, whenever required, most notably in the rasping string bass entries that underline the frantic jealousy of Golaud. The cast was dominated, not by the young hero and heroine (Henri Gui and Denise Duval), but by their elders: the tender and dignified Arkel of Guus Hoekman and the powerful and splendidly declaimed Golaud of Michel Roux; while Kerstin Meyer made a gravely beautiful Geneviève. Beni Montresor's designs provided an exquisitely harmonious counterpart to Carl Ebert's restrained yet powerful production. The cast was partly changed in the revival of the following year, and almost wholly new – with Ileana Cotrubas and Jill Gomez sharing the role of Mélisande – in that of 1969, which was conducted by John Pritchard and produced by Pierre Médecin.

And so to *La Bohème* in 1967. I nearly forgot it; for what, after all was *La Bohème* doing at Glyndebourne? No doubt the management felt like the German conductor who, when reproached for the conventional symphonic fare repeatedly offered in his programmes, loftily replied: 'I make it otherwise.' Glyndebourne was saying, in effect: 'You've seen *La Bohème*? Well, you haven't seen *us* do it!'

This was not the first time that the Sussex opera house had cast covetous eyes at the standard repertory. Ebert wanted to do *Carmen* and was deterred only by John Christie's notorious dislike of anything French. At one time there was talk of *La traviata*; and the *Barbiere di Siviglia* was actually smuggled in as part of the long Rossini series sponsored by Gui. But *La Bohème*, staple fare of every opera house in the world, was a surprising choice, to be justified, if at all, only by a performance of uncommon refinement and distinction. Such a performance was not achieved – at least in 1967: I did not venture back for the 1978 revival, which was newly directed with the old scenery by John Cox, and much better liked. The original production team had been that of the previous year's *Werther* – showing themselves rather less effective in the Italian work; the cast was not of festival standard. Nearly everyone sang too loudly. Hardly anyone remembered the intimate scale of the theatre; and there was little attempt to find such a natural, easy tone for the conversational exchanges of the opera as might alone have justified the curious enterprise.

So to the second and much smaller category of 'Other Operas': those that qualify for the description of modern, or at least recent. The first of these – severe critics of Glyndebourne will say, 'how typical!' – occupied only half an evening in 1966, when it was paired with Purcell's *Dido and Aeneas*. This was Ravel's *L'Heure espagnole*: a little jest that can easily misfire in the theatre, but which went very well on this occasion under John Pritchard, with sets by Osbert Lancaster and production by Dennis Maunder. The cast was strong, with Michel Sénéchal as an exquisitely affected and egotistic poet and Hugues Cuénod, a great Glynde-bourne favourite, as a lanky clockmaker-husband. As the so nearly unsatisfied heroine, Isabel Garcisanz sang with charming variety and displayed a wonderful reper-tory of apprehensive, dubious or disgusted looks. It is a pity that the opera has never come back – all the more so in that it goes so well with its still more delightful stablemate, *L'Enfant et les sortilèges*, a piece surely made for Glyndebourne.

A piece, on the other hand, that seemed very definite-ly *not* made for Glyndebourne was Gottfried von Einem's setting of Friedrich Dürrenmatt's *Visit of the Old Lady*, which reached the Sussex house in 1973 after having scored some success at its Vienna première of 1971 and elsewhere. The play is a black comedy, and the unoriginal music is skilfully put together, with touches of Carl Orff and Kurt Weill on the one hand, and of latter-day Strauss and even Massenet on the other. But the score is essentially heartless: never more so than when it is making a cunningly planned pretence at sweetness and charm. Kerstin Meyer's brilliant account of the title-role was marred by the frequent inaudibility of her English words. The opera, conducted by John Pritchard, produced by John Cox, and designed by Michael Annals, reappeared in the following season, but has since been dropped.

Allusion has already been made to Stravinsky's *The Rake's Progress*, which has proved to be the one sure-fire modern success in the Glyndebourne repertory. After its initial Edinburgh showing, it has been seen during seven seasons at Glyndebourne and on tour, reaching a grand total of seventy-eight performances. In its first four Glyndebourne seasons, the work had been entrusted to the experienced hands of Paul Sacher as conductor, Carl Ebert as producer, and Osbert Lancaster as designer; then came a twelve-year gap, and the opera reappeared in the enormously admired and original designs of David Hockney (effectively the start of his brilliant stage career), conducted by Bernard Haitink and produced by John Cox, with a strong cast headed by Jill Gomez as Anne, Leo Goeke as Tom, and Donald Gramm as Nick Shadow.

During the interval between the two incarnations of Stravinsky's *Rake*, Glyndebourne had twice ventured on really fresh ground. The first such choice, somewhat (as one is told) to John Christie's disgust, was, in 1961, Henze's *Elegy for Young Lovers*, to a libretto by W.H. Auden and Chester Kallman – the same team that had provided the text for *The Rake*. The opera had already been given abroad in German translation, but this was its first performance in the original English. Though providing some effective theatrical situations on which the composer had eagerly seized, it proved to be essentially an artificial concoction, containing moreover crudities of tone and diction that would have dismayed the fastidious stylist, Hugo von Hofmannsthal, to whom it is dedicated. The leading role of a supposedly great Austrian poet, the equal of Rilke or of Yeats, was disappointingly taken by Carlos Alexander after Paul Schöffler had at short notice dropped out, but there were some striking performances among the other parts, and effective staging by Günther Rennert in the brilliant decor of Lila de Nobili, while John Pritchard held together the complex score, which has not since been revived at Glyndebourne.

The second attempt at novelty was actually a Glyndebourne commission: Nicholas Maw's *The Rising of the Moon*, a romantic and occasionally farcical comedy about English soldiers garrisoned in the County Mayo of 1875. Beverly Cross's libretto and Maw's score amused, and sometimes touched, the Glyndebourne audiences of 1970; and the opera survived into the following season, by which time the composer had undertaken some extensive and badly needed pruning of his seriously over-written score, especially of its brass parts. But the actual composition still relied too much on harmonic and contrapuntal complexities, and too little on straightforward lyrical impulse, for the requirements of comic opera. It is an old lesson, which modern composers are most reluctant to learn. At all events, Glyndebourne did Maw's opera proud, with Colin Graham as producer, Osbert Lancaster as designer, and with a good cast under the direction originally of Raymond Leppard, and of Myer Fredman in 1971. An Oliver Knussen double bill based on Maurice Sendak short stories is planned for 1984.

A surprising, and promising, development was the very successful production of Janáček's *The Cunning Little Vixen* in 1975: by itself in the first year, and preceded by the Cocteau-Poulenc monologue, *La Voix humaine* (with Graziella Sciutti as the heroine in a new production designed by Martin Battersby) for its 1977 revival. As might have been foreseen (but not everyone would have guessed it), Janáček's utterly original forest idyll proved an instant Glyndebourne hit in the bold, yet poetical, production of Jonathan Miller with costumes and scenery by Rosemary Vercoe and Patrick Robertson respectively, while a cast led by Norma Burrowes as the Vixen and Benjamin Luxon as the Forester was accompanied by the London Philharmonic Orchestra, playing with particular sensitivity for Raymond Leppard.

Very sensibly, the opera was sung in Norman Tucker's
translation, not in some kind of phonetic Czech – which
makes it all the stranger that, when the next successful
attempt at Slavonic opera was made in 1982 with
Prokofiev's satirical *Love for Three Oranges* (in the
Haitink/Frank Corsaro/Maurice Sendak version) the
French translation should have been used, although in
comedy verbal clarity is especially important. I thought
the management was let off lightly for this *gaffe*, since
there was no possible excuse for using French except
that, at the Chicago première of 1921, a mainly French
company had made French translation seem a good idea.
In the autumn of 1983, however, the Glyndebourne
Touring Opera performed the Prokofiev opera in an
English translation commissioned from Tom Stoppard.

Slavonic opera, by the way, offers one of the most
likely fields for the refreshment of the Glyndebourne
repertory. Smetana's delightful *Two Widows* (for which
Strauss used to beg whenever business took him to
Prague), perhaps Dvorak's *Armida*, Rimsky-Korsakov's
magical *Snow Maiden* (not seen in England since long ago
at Sadler's Wells) and perhaps his *Invisible City of Kitezh* –
if that does not seem too large-scale for the house. But
the game of proposing one's personal favourites, at other
people's expense, is too tempting to be excessively
indulged.

Having contrived to miss *The Love for Three Oranges* (I
won't give it its French title!), I must end by confessing
to a more serious gap: I have not yet seen the universally
praised and enjoyed *Midsummer Night's Dream*, in which
the combined talents of Haitink, Peter Hall and John
Bury, together with a notable cast, effectively repaired in
1981 the somewhat slighting treatment that *The Rape of
Lucretia* had received at Glyndebourne so long before.
Relations between Glyndebourne and the English Opera
Group, which later formed the nucleus for the creation of

the Aldeburgh Festival, remained strained for some years, even though it was the EOG which gave the first performance of *Albert Herring* at Glyndebourne in the summer of 1947. When *Herring* returns to the repertory, as it is expected to do in 1985, another link in the Aldeburgh/Glyndebourne chain will have been re-forged.

The Discoveries

John Higgins

Glyndebourne generally prefers the home grown. There is clear evidence of this at the start of every season in the flower beds with the rows of young plants all raised from seed in the greenhouses leading towards the car park. As in the gardens, so in the house. It has been a rearing ground for young talent for a good quarter of a century now. It has been a natural start, always assuming of course that you can impress the selection committee, for aspirant singers, opera producers and even arts administrators. A spell at Glyndebourne on the *curriculum vitae* has long been reckoned an excellent thing. The house has been accused of being 'a club' by those who have not adapted to the conditions there. But among those who have fitted in there is usually extreme loyalty and that loyalty tends to be reciprocal.

In the beginning, while it was still learning its trade, Glyndebourne had to be an importer of talent. Fritz Busch and Carl Ebert, soon to be joined by Rudolf Bing, brought with them central European expertise in the day-to-day running of an opera house, something which certainly did not exist in Sussex. Naturally enough they brought with them too some of the artists they had been working with in Germany and Austria. As Glyndebourne re-established itself after the war, so it moved gradually from being an importer into becoming an exporter as well.

Glyndebourne's first major 'export' was probably Bing himself, who left to run the Metropolitan Opera House in New York, via the Edinburgh Festival. One of the first men to be engaged by Bing as an assistant was Ian Hunter, who had happened to have a brief spell on Busch's music staff in the pre-war days, another example of the Glyndebourne connection having its influence. Hunter, an aspirant conductor turned administrator, was to follow Bing at the Edinburgh Festival and then to take over the direction of Britain's oldest concert management company, Harold Holt.

In those early post-war days there were not many places to go for those who wanted to be involved in opera, either front stage or back stage. Covent Garden was struggling to find its new identity, Sadler's Wells struggling to establish one. The Carl Rosa was beginning to look increasingly tacky and the death clouds were beginning to hover over it. There were no regional companies until the Welsh National Opera was established in Cardiff in the early 1950s. So Glyndebourne was the selected place for many of those with the sharpest eye on the future. It is no surprise to find that John Cox, who was named Glyndebourne's first director of production in 1972, had earlier put in six successive summers there on the staff, working first with Carl Ebert himself and then with Günther Rennert.

As far as the singers were concerned, during the 1950s a pattern was established of mixing international artists – among them Simoneau, Valdengo and Simionato – plus some who were just establishing themselves, such as Nilsson and Tajo, with those who can correctly be described as Glyndebourne 'discoveries'. The Vienna links were particularly strong both through Ebert's and Busch's old contacts as well as through Jani Strasser, the long-serving head of music staff. And the house was lucky enough to have the right ears in the right place: in vocal terms Vienna was making better music than any other city in Europe. It was a period particularly rich in sopranos and among the visitors were Lisa Della Casa, Ljuba Welitsch, Hilde Güden, Sari Barabas and, above all, Sena Jurinac who did not miss a season between 1949 and 1956. All were part of the great Vienna revival and it was a list any opera house could have been well satisfied with, but among the well-known names Ebert and Glyndebourne's general manager, Moran Caplat, were filtering in some new ones.

Again it is the sopranos who stand out. In 1956 Joan Sutherland, who had been struggling to find her form and vocal identity at Covent Garden, was cast as the Countess in *Figaro*, a role she had sung for the London company but only on tour. Sutherland was to keep up her Sussex links for a few seasons, culminating in her marvellous Elvira in *Puritani* in 1960. But Glyndebourne's most important signing of this period was surely Elisabeth Söderström, who started off her career almost as a mezzo. Her first two Glyndebourne parts were the Composer in *Ariadne* (in 1957) and Octavian in *Rosenkavalier* (in 1959) and an association between singer and opera house was started which was to last over twenty years. Without Miss Söderström Glyndebourne would probably never have embarked on the Strauss cycle, directed by John Cox, of the 1970s. Another key name of the late 1950s is that of Teresa Berganza, who made her British début at Glyndebourne as Cherubino in 1958, following it up with the title role in *La cenerentola* a season later.

The influence of Vittorio Gui, who eventually was appointed head of music in 1960, began to be felt more and more, especially on the Italian repertoire. Gui had been used as a consultant by Busch back in the earliest days of Glyndebourne and became very much the house's Italian connection. The Vienna scene was fully surveyed, so part of Gui's job was to report on what was available in Italy. It was an occupation for which he was excellently suited, not only because of his own conducting commitments within Italy but also through the strongest of family links with the opera business. Gui had a great success with one of his earliest 'introductions', Graziella Sciutti as Rosina in *Il barbiere*, and encouraged by this he made sure that Glyndebourne acquired the new generation of Italian singers before they became too well-known and, consequently, expensive.

And once again it was the choice of sopranos which proved to be the most astute. Ilva Ligabue arrived in 1958 to sing Alice in *Falstaff*, a role in which many of us reckon she had no superior in the subsequent quarter of a century. A year later Gui suggested that a young girl called Mirella Freni should be auditioned, which she duly was in Milan. Everyone reckoned she would be a good Zerlina and this was the role she was given at Glyndebourne in 1960 and one which she made her own for some years thereafter. Luigi Alva, who was to sing opposite Freni in Zeffirelli's magical production of *L'elisir d'amore* very shortly afterwards, was found at roughly the same time at the Holland Festival. And there was too Régine Crespin, yet another singer to make her British stage début at Glyndebourne, as the Marschallin in *Rosenkavalier*, in this period when top quality sopranos were there for the picking, if only you knew where to find them.

The appointment of Günther Rennert in 1960 as head of production meant that Germany once again featured on the list of countries which Glyndebourne had well covered on its scouting network. In addition, its own staff, led by Moran Caplat, made forays to the continent during the autumn and winter when the house was closed, often going to quite small theatres to build up the casts for the future. Kerstin Meyer was introduced via Elisabeth Söderström; Edith Mathis at the very start of her career had a successful audition in Cologne and was engaged; Reri Grist, who had abandoned her native New York for the German opera houses, took the soubrette roles of Despina and Zerbinetta; Ingvar Wixell, who was totally unknown in Britain at this time, was Guglielmo in a *Così* (1962), which was not as good as it should have been. But the real discovery was almost certainly not a singer, a conductor or even an administrator but a new type of operatic sound, as far as Glyndebourne and most of the rest of Britain was concerned, in the shape of Monteverdi's *L'incoronazione di Poppea* arranged by Raymond Leppard. The story of that opera is told in Raymond Leppard's own chapter.

During the mid-1960s the casting went off the boil. The flair of a decade ago had disappeared and there were too many routine engagements. The exception was *Idomeneo* (1964) which brought together Luciano Pavarotti and Gundula Janowitz for their sole Glyndebourne appearances and one of their very rare operatic partnerships. Spike Hughes in his book *Glyndebourne*, is quick to point out that Pavarotti was signed in Sussex before he had appeared either at La Scala or at Covent Garden, although the audition took place at the latter house.

It was about this time that Glyndebourne began to realise that they did not have to rely on their scouting system abroad, or indeed on Central Casting in the case of some of the more familiar operas, to pick their singers. There was now a source on their doorstep in the shape of the Glyndebourne Chorus. Just as the young producers and administrators had reckoned that a spell in Sussex made an excellent start to a career, so a place in the Chorus was the right stepping stone for those just out of music college, quite apart from being an exceptionally pleasant way of passing the summer.

The most famous alumnus of the Glyndebourne Chorus was Janet Baker, who had spent a couple of seasons there back in the mid-1950s. She returned in 1966, as Dido in a performance of Purcell's opera which remains engraved on the memory. Perhaps by co-incidence 1964 was the *annus mirabilis* of the Glynde-bourne Chorus, which contained among other young singers Ryland Davies, Richard Van Allan and Anne Howells. By 1966 they were all reckoned good enough to be assigned small parts in the season's repertory: all got into *Die Zauberflöte*, while Davies made a brief appear-ance in that *Dido and Aeneas* with Janet Baker. Was Glyndebourne the cradle for the rebirth of British singing which was just about to occur? Or was it the Royal Northern College of Music from which both Anne Howells and Ryland Davies came? That is open to argument. Perhaps the Royal Northern College was the cradle and Glyndebourne the nursery. For years the representation of British opera abroad had been spear-headed mainly by Geraint Evans, who had hardly missed a Glyndebourne season throughout the 1950s, but in the future he was going to be joined by one or two of his compatriots including those of Ringmer's class of '64.

Almost certainly the success of the young British contingent in this and the following two seasons was one of the reasons for the formation of the Glyndebourne Touring Opera, which is properly the concern of Gillian Widdicombe's chapter. But the antennae were well tuned: it was realised that there was not just the odd native-born voice worth cultivating but a whole gener-ation likely to change the pattern of British singing. To

the trio already mentioned there has to be added
Margaret Price, who was never part of the Chorus but
who can be put in that special year of '66 because she
appeared as the Angel in *Jephtha*. Handel's opera might
have provided Glyndebourne with one of its dullest
evenings of the last quarter century, but those with ears
pricked them up at Miss Price's contribution and no one
was surprised to find her back in the more rewarding role
of Constanze (*Die Entführung*) a couple of years later and
then as Fiordiligi in *Così*.

In the late 1960s the most interesting of the young
artists to be heard tended to be either British born or
trained. The two exceptions to this generality were
perhaps a couple of tenors: the American George Shir-
ley, whose engagement as Tamino led to a longish
association with the house, and the Italian Ugo Benelli,
who had been recommended by Gui and auditioned
(favourably) in Italy as long ago as 1959 but obtained his
first Glyndebourne part as Nemorino (*L'elisir d'amore*) on
the basis of a big success at the Wexford Festival. Close
links between the festivals in Sussex and South-East
Ireland were building up at this time: regular foraging
parties went over each October to the Wexford Festival
and it was no surprise to find Brian Dickie and John Cox,
old Glyndebourne hands, working there as respectively
artistic director and one of the best of the regular
producers. Dickie, as he moved up the Glyndebourne
ranks, became the chief talent scout for the house and
found himself quite quickly acting as 'artistic adviser' for
a number of theatres on the continent and especially for
those in France.

Back in Sussex it was also the policy to buy British and
to interlard the new generation with a number of
seasoned hands from Europe, both east and west. There
were those who reckoned that imports from the eastern
bloc had been somewhat overdone, and they had a

point. The class of '64 had done well in *Die Entführung* –
an appropriate enough opera for the young Turks to
show their paces – and Ryland Davies was back in the
1969 *Così*, this time with Anne Howells as one of his
partners. Stafford Dean, another ex-member of the
Chorus, repeated his Bailiff in *Werther* before going off
for a lengthy spell of singing Mozart on the continent,
although he was of course to return several years later as
Leporello in Peter Hall's famous production of *Don
Giovanni* and Alfonso in the same director's *Così*.
Leporello in 1969 was yet another member of that class
of '64: Richard Van Allan.

There was however one person from Eastern Europe
who was welcomed with delight in 1969, Ileana Cotrubas. Moran Caplat and George Christie had heard her
in Scheveningen as Gilda a couple of years earlier; her
waif-like features and the purity of her soprano gave her
instant success as Mélisande and it was obvious that she
was going to take roughly the same position in Glyndebourne's communal heart as Elisabeth Söderström. She
was a natural for the Sussex house, extremely pretty and
a first-rate actress – no less could be expected from a
family with close connections with the stage. After
Mélisande her chief successes at Glyndebourne were all
to come in Peter Hall productions: in the title role of *La
Calisto*, Hall's first opera here, Susanna in *Figaro* and
most recently Tytania in *A Midsummer Night's Dream*.
Sciutti ... Freni ... Söderström ... Cotrubas ...
Glyndebourne have a knack of getting their sopranos
right. And perhaps their bass-baritones too, because
Ruggero Raimondi was there as Don Giovanni, a role he
was beginning to sing in the Italian opera houses,
including Venice.

Peter Hall can hardly be classified as a Glyndebourne
'discovery', but when he decided against joining the
administration of Covent Garden Glyndebourne was

swift to forge closer links with him. His first and very successful Glyndebourne production, *La Calisto* (1970), has led to an association with the house which has culminated in Hall's becoming the present artistic director. From this rapid switch of opera houses Glyndebourne began to see the next decade taking some kind of shape: Hall after his two excursions into baroque opera with Leppard, *La Calisto* and *Il ritorno d'Ulisse*, was to be in charge of a Mozart cycle, while John Cox, who could more reasonably be called one of their own, was simultaneously to turn his attention to Richard Strauss. But before the full Hall-Cox influence was felt there was one last fling in the early 1970s into Eastern Europe, which produced in 1971 Teresa Kubiak as Lisa in *The Queen of Spades* and Sylvia Geszty as Zerbinetta (*Ariadne*) and a little later Edita Gruberova (Queen of the Night in *Die Zauberflöte*), all brilliant performances which proved that the east was really worth trawling after all. All three sopranos were making their British débuts, as indeed had Cotrubas a few years earlier.

Glyndebourne for the first time in its history was running with a British artistic administration, with John Pritchard and John Cox as musical director and production director respectively and Peter Hall taking a proprietory interest in the works he was staging. Some artists were engaged who had been making their names principally at Covent Garden, not previously one of Glyndebourne's favourite sources: Kiri Te Kanawa (the Countess in *Figaro*), as well as Robert Lloyd (Sarastro in *Die Zauberflöte*). Attention was turned chiefly to English-speaking singers and especially those from America, which was proving to have the kind of renaissance that Britain had had in the 1960s.

Glyndebourne's Columbus-like look towards the New World has managed to yield so far a notable singer almost every year, starting with James Morris (Banquo in

Macbeth, 1972), Frederica von Stade (Cherubino in *Figaro*, 1973), Barbara Hendricks as *La Calisto* (1974). In 1976 John Pritchard introduced Calvin Simmons, who died miserably young in a boating accident in 1982, as conductor of *Figaro* and Samuel Ramey who took the title role well before his international career began. Ashley Putnam (Musetta in *Bohème*), Maria Ewing (Dorabella in *Così*) continued that tradition in 1978, as indeed did Kathleen Battle in Haydn's *La fedeltà premiata* the following year. It was considered that the Haydn vein was not worth mining further despite some quite powerful voices in favour. But the American one was and it yielded Faith Esham as Cherubino (*Figaro*) in 1981 and Carol Vaness as an outstanding Donna Anna (*Don Giovanni*, 1982) and Electra (*Idomeneo*, 1983).

America had taken over from Europe, despite the appearance of sopranos such as Lucia Aliberti, another Wexford import, as Nanetta in the 1980 *Falstaff*. And the reasons reflected the strengths and weaknesses of the Glyndebourne scouting system. John Cox was working frequently in the United States, mainly outside New York, while John Pritchard was regularly engaged in San Francisco. Naturally enough their proposals were related more often than not to the artists with whom they were working and by good chance it happened at a time when America was fast de-centralising its opera and there was plenty of work in Santa Fe, Houston, Seattle and a whole circuit of houses far removed from Manhattan. Glyndebourne had become a kind of English-speaking union, whereas a few years previously English was just about the last language to be heard underneath the arches or in the staff canteen. A glance down the cast list of the 1977 *Così* reveals only one role, Fiordiligi, not cast with a singer brought up to speak English. And the conductor, Bernard Haitink? Well, his English has been well-nigh perfect for some years now.

Although George Christie and Brian Dickie were now much more likely to hold their auditions in New York or San Francisco than in Milan or Bucharest there was a full realisation that the Chorus was still providing a steady flow of performers who would be taking principal roles at Glyndebourne and internationally. Thomas Allen moved up this way to appear in some of the *Figaro* performances in 1974 and, of course, *Don Giovanni* some years later; David Rendall had a year in the Chorus and a tiny part in the 1976 *Onegin* before he became Ferrando (*Così*); and John Rawnsley followed a similar pattern before Masetto in the Hall *Giovanni* and the title part of *Il barbiere*. Others won their successes with the Touring Company, notably Linda Esther Gray and Felicity Lott, before they achieved principal parts at the Summer Festival.

In the future, or at least the immediate one, Glyndebourne seems likely to turn its eyes inwards rather than outwards both with singers and conductors – and it is worth recording that Andrew Davis conducted his first opera at Glyndebourne and that Simon Rattle obtained his early experience with the GTO and conducted his first festival performances in 1977 when he was only twenty-two. But it has had a good record of placing its ears where the talent is and in the second half of the 1980s that might not necessarily be in Britain. It is also under a historic obligation to introduce a world-class soprano every few years: perhaps in Carol Vaness it has.

Inevitably, this selection of discoveries has to be a personal one, based primarily on season by season visits to Glyndebourne now spanning almost a quarter of a century. Others will surely offer different candidates, particularly from the 1950s, a period when Glyndebourne was only accessible to me through broadcasts. But our joint wish must be that the house keeps its ears and eyes wide open both front stage and back stage.

The Rule of Taste
Design at Glyndebourne, 1935-84

Roy Strong

By its very nature opera design tends to be conservative. The history of design at Glyndebourne over the last fifty years is as interesting a case study as any in this conservatism. Scenery and costumes for an opera production are a major investment. They can be a costly mistake, particularly in terms of the soaring prices of today. All the pressures, therefore, are to be cautious and to be safe. This may strike a very dull note at the opening of an account of design at Glyndebourne but I feel it strikes a very true one. The opera companies with public subsidy can be (they rarely are) far more adventurous in terms of design than one which depends on continued support and applause from an audience whose aesthetic attitudes are so readily classifiable.

I start with the box office because what a Glyndebourne audience expects in design is enchantment, delight, spectacle and wit. They do not expect to be shocked by vulgarity, crudity or visual barbarism. They would not warm to a *Così fan tutte* set in a railway siding or a production of *I puritani* in which cavaliers and roundheads are updated into terms of the Conservative and Labour parties. It was noticeable, for example, that the occasional introduction of nudity in the 1970s was indifferently received. That the audience is largely made up of the well-off professional middle classes bent on culture in comfort rather than impoverished opera buffs is a commonplace. The age group too, tends to be over rather than under forty. There is, therefore, always a time lag in visual taste to take into account which successive administrators at Glyndebourne over the last thirty years have very shrewdly judged. The point can easily be made by saying that the right moment to have asked David Hockney to have designed an opera was in the mid-1960s. In fact he was not asked until 1975 by which time he had assumed a place in the British art scene comparable to that of Lord Leighton or G.F. Watts. The same could be said of John Bury's work which might have been anathema to opera audiences in the 1960s, although he designed both *Moses und Aron* and *Die Zauberflöte* for Covent Garden. By the 1970s his approach had become a norm of production in the classic theatre with a school of imitators attached to it. In terms of the history of the rest of theatre, however, this approach was by then almost old-fashioned, although in those of Glyndebourne and of opera in general, it seemed revolutionary. On the whole therefore the aim of every Glyndebourne production, in common with most other opera houses, has been to achieve a classic and only to take in the *avant garde* once its new vocabulary of vision had been widely learned and acclaimed as acceptable. In several cases Glyndebourne has been ahead of other houses in making a new step forward.

The earliest designer to work at Glyndebourne was the unmemorable Hamish Wilson. He came upon the scene by way of Audrey Mildmay and the Carl Rosa Opera. Totally untrained as an artist, he had previously designed for the British National Opera Company. He was obviously a great favourite with the Christies, whose visual awareness certainly in no way matched their musical. Wilson was in on the creation of the opera house from the start and it is clear that whether the in-coming conductor or producer liked his work or not his role as designer was to be part of the deal. It is difficult to think that Ebert, who later showed a marked interest in designers, can ever have been satisfied with Wilson. One only knows his work from photographs and a couple of feeble set drawings which have recently emerged from the attics of Glyndebourne. He designed sets for five Mozart operas and Donizetti's *Don Pasquale* which had a life spanning the period 1934–48. It would be a distortion of the truth to say anything other than that these sets would have been more appropriate to touring productions of musicals by Ivor Novello than fit to grace an operatic stage. Nor were British designers lacking at that date: Motley, Cecil Beaton, Rex Whistler and Oliver Messel had all essayed their first work in the theatre in or about 1935. An adventurous design policy was not part of the initial Glyndebourne concept and indeed as one strolls through the unchanged interior of the house today with its pseudo-baronial country house décor, absolutely safe, old-master furniture, pictures and tapestries, there is nothing to indicate that either John or Audrey Christie had a flicker of an interest in contemporary art or design. This is a feature which they have in common with most music enthusiasts and critics to this day.

There were obviously some intractable technical conditions under which any in-coming designer would have had to have laboured in the first two years. These were rectified in 1936: a scenery tower was built thus enabling cloths to be flown and, by removing the back wall of the stage, the depth of it was virtually doubled from the footlights from 29 to 59 feet. In 1938 Neher was engaged for *Macbeth*. He had worked with Busch and Ebert on their production of *Un ballo in maschera* at Charlottenburg in 1932, and his designs for *Don Giovanni* had been seen at Covent Garden in 1936. His drawings alone establish him in a different class from Wilson. They are at once professional and not amateur, monumental in concept with dramatic perspective and *chiaroscuro* effects. The history of design proper at Glyndebourne begins with Neher and not with Wilson.

When Glyndebourne embarked on its great revival in the post-1950 period, it was marked by a significant change of attitude to design. It would be interesting to know what prompted this. As Hamish Wilson had mercifully faded from the scene it must have been that Ebert could at last, as a disciple of Max Reinhardt, reveal his true colours. Or had John Christie awoken to all that had happened during the war years to British design? It is noticeable that virtually all the designers of the emergent new period owed their first commissions to Ninette de Valois and Robert Helpmann for productions for the Sadler's Wells Ballet. Although Oliver Messel had worked in the theatre in the 1930s, his most important contributions had been *Comus* (1942) and *The Sleeping Beauty* (1946). Leslie Hurry, soon to design *La forza del destino* for Glyndebourne (1951), was a Helpmann discovery designing the famous war-time *Hamlet* (1942) and *Swan Lake* (1943). Osbert Lancaster, commissioned to design the *Rake's Progress* for Glyndebourne (1953), first entered the theatre with Cranko's ballet *Pineapple Poll* in 1951 and John Piper, who designed *Don Giovanni* for Glyndebourne in 1951, had first essayed theatre in Ashton's war-time ballet *The Quest* in 1943.

All these gave design at Glyndebourne in the 1950s a strongly British slant. It was a period of continuing austerity when sumptuous effects had to be obtained by the minimum resources and maximum inventiveness.

It was an era in which the new synthetic materials had yet to arrive to revolutionise set construction. Throughout the 1950s we are still in the age of canvas flats and painted cloths, of illusion achieved through painterliness. There is also little evidence of the recognition of all that had happened in set design since Diaghilev to assimilate abstractionism and other modernist movements in the visual arts. Generally it would be true to say that the designers were exponents of an insular neo-romantic tradition.

Of all these designers none seemed more conducive to Ebert's vision than Oliver Messel. From the visual point of view the decade 1950–60 was Messel's decade. His *Figaro* (1955) was revived even in 1965 and he collaborated with Ebert on no fewer than nine productions, a figure equalled so far only by John Bury. Why did this relationship work? The answer lies back in the 1930s, for Messel had worked with Ebert's master, Max von Reinhardt, designing the costumes for a revival of *The Miracle* (1932). Messel's vision was still a pre-war one. It was 1930s' neo-romanticism of a type exemplified by the Sitwells' cult of the rococo, Cecil Beaton's photographs of the Queen Mother in the manner of Winterhalter or the paintings of Rex Whistler. Messel's was a gossamer world of gilded enchantment, always bent on lifting the subject matter of his design away from reality. No other designer, whose work I can remember, has ever given his audience better rose-coloured spectacles through which to peer at the past. He presented Mozart as through the eyes of Gainsborough and Fragonard. His sets were transparent watercolours of infinite subtlety, on to which he splashed highlights of crimson and gold. And there was always an innate feeling for elegance and restraint mingled with a brilliant ability to conjure up splendour but never vulgarity. Messel, with his parents' home at nearby Nymans and his upper-class English

connections, was perfectly cast for the Glyndebourne of
the 1950s.

Messel's approach was consistent and can be followed
in production after production. He avoided monumen-
tality which would never have worked on the small stage
of Glyndebourne. He always carefully framed each
production into a special proscenium of irregularly
swagged, rich drapery, behind which he worked in terms
of a toy theatre world with a strong sense of diminutive
grandeur and domestic refinement. It was a world
viewed from the Petit Trianon and Marie Antoinette
would have felt at home in any of his settings. The
Countess floats in pale pink panniers in the last set of
Figaro (1955) across a garden of feathery grey-green trees
towards a treillage pavilion. A year later we see the same
ingredients with an oriental twist for *Die Entführung.*
This time the set is flanked by trellis and drapery but
these frame orderly rows of cypress trees, a golden palm
and treillage pavilions in the oriental manner. Even the
chorus of inmates of the harem are in panniers. It is
important to point out that the tradition was followed
exactly in the work of two of his young assistants. Carl
Toms' designs for the set of *Il segreto di Susanna* (1959)
and Anthony Powell's costumes for *Capriccio* (1963) are
so close in manner that they could be mistaken for his
work. Both designers were later to achieve distinction
but their own style had yet to be formed.

Along with Messel, there were two other designers
who were purely an insular taste: Hugh Casson and
Osbert Lancaster. Casson, who had *via* the Festival of
Britain made certain aspects of the modernist movement
acceptable and even fun to the post-war establishment
classes, was to return to the Glyndebourne stage over a
period of thirty years. His first opera was *Alceste* (1953)
and his last Haydn's *La fedeltà premiata* (1979). His stage
style did not change over the years. Essentially architec-

tural, it owed much to the work of Edward Gordon Craig but was overlaid by Scandinavian influences. Lancaster is a more complex phenomenon. His genius lies in sending up the establishment without threatening it. His twopence coloured flat cartoon style is unexportable, the allusions would sink, like those in a Betjeman poem, mid-Channel. But for a Glyndebourne audience, made up largely of the people he at once caricatures and reassures, Lancaster was the perfect foil to offset the cerebral musical demands of new operas. His first opera was Stravinsky's *The Rake's Progress* (1953) and his last Nicholas Maw's *The Rising of the Moon* (1970). Regardless of whom the opera is by, we are found visually to be firmly in Drayneflete at some period of its past with members of the Littlehampton family *en charade*. It is a formula that can work successfully in the theatre in only very exceptional circumstances and perhaps his *Falstaff* (1955) with its 'Ideal Homes' Elizabethan scenery, so remote from anything that Verdi could ever have envisaged, struck the right note for the early years of the new Elizabethan age.

Messel, Casson and Lancaster do not cover all the strands of the 1950s but they certainly set the dominant visual style: romantic, rather old-fashioned, patriotic but with touches of Festival of Britain modernism. The mood of the Günther Rennert era (1960–7) was to be a very different one. It was for the first time, on a noticeable scale, international, and the leading designer was an Italian, Emanuele Luzzati, who designed no fewer than six productions between 1963 and 1970 for Franco Enriquez. The visual change can be established by looking at his designs for *Die Entführung* (1968) in comparison with those by Oliver Messel. The sense of wit and spectacle are there but the optical sense is abstract, an approach to theatre design new to Glyndebourne but stretching back to Diaghilev's designers, notably in Luzzati's case, to Gontcharova. Luzzati conceives his peopled scenes not as misty, romantic visions from another world based on renaissance optical principles but as shifting patterns of colour and light like a moving Byzantine mosaic. In these productions Glyndebourne audiences were moved on to an acceptable abstractionism.

Not that the romantic streak was abandoned. It can never be as long as classic operas need to be revived in terms of their own age. The 1960s brought Franco Zefferelli (1961), Lila da Nobili (1961) and her protégés, Beni Montresor, and Henry Bardon with David Walker (1966 and 1967). Stemming basically from Visconti, this was a romanticism far different from Messel's. Its aim was a *verismo* in theatre based on traditions of scene-painting from the nineteenth century but now allied to all the new light-weight construction materials that enabled a three-dimensional reality of a kind, totally unknown before, to take the stage. Every character in the chorus was assigned a character and a costume, and the effect at its best was of a heightened reality of another world designed to meet the challenge of a new generation of audiences who, through films, and now through television, was not only visually better educated but could not accept the two-dimensional premise of the earlier approach. Audiences now saw in three dimensions. Henry Bardon's attic for the first scene of *La Bohème* (1967) catches the re-animated archaeological mood exactly, arranged as a box set with a steep fake perspective to the huge studio windows overlooking Paris. Every single square foot is covered by peeling paint and wallpaper, damaged woodwork and cracked windows.

If the 1950s were the Messel decade, the 1970s were John Bury's. The arrival of Peter Hall in 1970 meant the advent of Bury with whom he had always worked. The approach was to be radically different from anything yet experienced by Glyndebourne audiences, productions whose thrust was both intellectual and sociological. Exactness of period mood and re-creation has little part in this visual philosophy whose aim is to emphasise a particular interpretation of an opera both in terms of its statement within its own age but more especially in terms of today. Eight productions in all have been essayed so far by this formidable team and only in one does enchantment in the old sense seem to have provided the main motivation, the magical moving glittering wood in Britten's *A Midsummer Night's Dream* (1981). By far their most important contribution, however, has been to make live for a modern audience the power and passion of early Baroque opera. In the hands of the neo-romantic designers these had always been presented as pastiches of Baroque theatre. Bury, under the inspiration of Hall, stripped away this fairy tinsel and in *La Calisto* (1970) and *Il ritorno d'Ulisse in patria* (1972) presented the guts of Baroque theatre in terms of late twentieth-century vision. In the second, three great tramlines receded back in perspective through the heavens and along this track soared the deities. By exposing and not concealing the mechanisms of the stage heaven, far from diminishing its power, it re-established it in the eyes of the onlooker. The audience re-experienced the same sense of wonder and awe that was the essence of such theatre. It was a formula less successfully applied to Gluck's *Orfeo* (1982). Indeed the latter was a lost opportunity, for Hall and Bury who had come up with so satisfactory a solution for Baroque opera should never have applied it in the first place to what is recognised as a landmark of neo-classicism.

The origins of this approach to production and design were, of course, far different from those of Ebert. They stem directly from the work of Karl von Appens for the Berliner Ensemble in the post-war period. Bury's beginnings as a designer for Joan Littlewood at the Stratford

East Theatre fit neatly into this ideological pattern. It is an interesting comment on the British establishment that a type of production whose roots were so revolutionary and left-wing, should within a generation be ensconced safely as an acceptable format within that bastion of the establishment, Glyndebourne. Nothing bears this out more readily than the three Mozart productions and the one of Beethoven. The rose-coloured spectacles of Messel and the fantasy of Luzzati, were replaced by a much more humdrum, grey, Welfare State approach. The Count's house in *Figaro* (1973) is not an enchanting rococo pavilion, but a rather down-at-heel seedy place where it would not be difficult for servant and master relationships to become muddled. The garden in the last act was not graced by elegant gazebos but by plastic grass. The designer in each instance gave his producer what he wanted: an architectural framework into which he could move his cast flexibly and emphasise character, class and relationship. The latter two had to be defined more by acting than by costume, for Bury's designs deliberately eschew any historical knowledge beyond a vague silhouette. In terms of production the Hall–Bury relationship has given us some of the most thought-provoking evenings at Glyndebourne but they have not given or attempted to give delight in terms of design.

Delight is, however, an attribute as old as theatre and it is the interest in design of John Cox (who took over as Director of Production in 1972) that has provided us with the visual feast of the last few years. Cox was an assistant to Ebert. In this case, the stance *vis-à-vis* Hall is so extreme in the opposite direction that from design becoming almost incidental it has on occasion been in danger of becoming the central ingredient of several productions. It was, however, a coup to persuade the already opera-struck Hockney to design Stravinsky's *Rake's Progress* (1975). It was, in addition, a brave one, for however brilliant the designs the onlooker will constantly have been irritated by what seemed the designer's lack of technical knowlege resulting in lengthy intervals to change the sets. Nor was he, whose aim was to reduce everyone to a line engraving, able to control after the first night the make-up of the chorus. None the less it was the first time since John Piper's *Don Giovanni* that a leading contemporary painter had been invited to design at Glyndebourne. In the intervening years stage design as a profession which demands special technical training and skills had grown so enormously that the crossing from canvas to stage was not the easy one it had been in Diaghilev's day. Although Hockney's *Die Zauberflöte* (1978) showed a marked advance in how to change scenery by sticking to flat, painted cloths the ability successfully to light them was never achieved. On the whole, however, Hockney's vibrant colour and exactness of line provided pure pleasure as audiences revelled in each delightful trick of the eye.

Cox's period has taken us out of the 1970s and into the 1980s with productions often heavily sold on their design. He began with two productions notable for their wit, observation and style, Martin Battersby's *Capriccio* (1973) and *Intermezzo* (1974). Erté's *Rosenkavalier* (1980) was in many ways a catastrophe, a perverse use of Erté's talents which are so pure an expression of art deco. To move the setting on virtually a century did not help, in addition to which, Erté, used to designing for dancers, whose bodies are perfect, made no allowances for the irregularities of the singers. The designs made up a beautiful portfolio of drawings but as costumes to be sung in, the results were less than fortunate.

The second production was Prokofiev's *The Love for Three Oranges* (1982) with designs by the American illustrator, Maurice Sendak, teamed up with the stage director with whom he had regularly worked, Frank

Corsaro. It can certainly be said of these that they greatly enhanced what is not Prokofiev's finest work. The approach was not so different from that of Hockney, making great use of painted cloths and cut-outs. Both artists are, of course, graphic ones and it is difficult for them to think in anything but two-dimensional terms so that in the long run their work – like that of Osbert Lancaster – can only successfully be applied in limited circumstances.

How am I to sum up? By now the reader may think that I am hyper-critical. I am. Glyndebourne will always be in a 'Catch 22' situation for those who run it. In the field of design their genius has been to know the moment when to press the button for some new kind of visual experience. Their role is not to cut new ground but to be an ultimate accolade. Glyndebourne has to reassure its audiences not shatter them. Recession, like war, tends to make people even safer than they would normally be and change in the arts awaits financial buoyancy. Working on the time lapse and if austerity continues, by the close of the 1980s, Glyndebourne could see productions of extreme simplicity, put together in the main from what is to hand. These in their way are anti-design and one stream in the theatre views money spent on scenery and costumes with a distaste that is almost ideological. Sooner or later this 'theatre workshop' approach to productions will be inevitable by the sheer force of the fact that a young generation brought up to the happy-go-lucky theatre-in-the-round approach will become the new Glyndebourne audience. The new radical chic always replaces the old.

But there are probably more serious problems. To meet the needs of everything that will happen in opera within the next fifty years, the Glyndebourne stage will have to be rebuilt. It has already reached the limits of its optical possibilities. The strains of containing manifold theatrical traditions within one form of stage has already broken down. It requires three types of stage at the National Theatre to meet modern requirements. By the close of the 1980s I therefore predict a remodelling of the stage at Glyndebourne in a more flexible form designed to handle both the classic and contemporary repertoire in a far more imaginative way than the inflexible peep-hole through which we have peered so often and with such pleasure for the last half century.

Beginnings

1 Hamish Wilson, design for *Così fan tutte*, 1934. Wilson's designs epitomise the almost amateur standard of design when' Glyndebourne began

2 Caspar Neher, *Un ballo in maschera* (1949). Neher was the first international designer to work at Glyndebourne

Neo-Romanticism of the 1950s: Oliver Messel

3 *Opposite, above left*: costume design for *La cenerentola* (1952)
4 *Opposite, above right*: costume design for Dr Bartolo in *Il barbiere* (1954)
5 *Opposite, below*: set design for *La cenerentola* (1952)
6 *Above*: model for the set of *Die Entführung aus dem Serail* (1956)

Two idiosyncratic British designers of the 1950s

7   Hugh Casson, *Alceste* (1953), Act III

8   Osbert Lancaster, *Falstaff* (1955), Act II, Scene I

1960s Abstractionism: Emanuele Luzzati

9   *Right*: costume design for
     Macbeth (1964)
10 *Below, left*: costume design
     for the three boys, *Die
     Zauberflöte* (1963)
11 *Below, right*: costume design
     for Leporello, *Don Giovanni*
     (1967)
12 *On the next page*: *Die
     Entführung* (1968) set design

LUZZATI 67

Romantic *verismo* of the 1960s

13   Franco Zeffirelli, *L'elisir d'amore* (1961), Act I, Scene I

14   Henry Bardon, *Werther* (1966), Act I, Scene I, set design

1970s Brutalism: John Bury

15   *La Calisto* (1970), costume
design

16   *Il ritorno d'Ulisse in patria*
(1972), model for the set

Graphics into Stage Design: David Hockney

17 *The Rake's Progress* (1975), Act II, Scene III, Tom's morning
room

18 *Die Zauberflöte* (1978), Act I, Scene I

19　*Der Rosenkavalier* (1980), design for Act II, Scene I

Three-Dimensional Stage Design: Maurice Sendak

20   Prokofiev, *Love for Three Oranges* (1982), Act III, Scene II

Mozart at Glyndebourne half a century ago

Isaiah Berlin

I wish I could say that I was a member of that small company which, drawn by friendship, curiosity, hope, or simple faith, boarded the historic train which went from Victoria to Sussex in May 1934, for the inaugural performance of *Le nozze di Figaro*. Nor, I am ashamed to say, did I go in 1935. I thought only about the Salzburg Festival, which I visited every year from 1929 until the Anschluss. I was not, before the war, as I now am, an addicted reader of periodicals, and had simply not taken in the new musical phenomenon. Nobody I spoke to at Oxford, where I lived as undergraduate and don, so much as mentioned Glyndebourne's existence before 1936 at the earliest. Yet I did not move in wholly philistine circles.

In 1936 I did go to Glyndebourne, and heard a performance of *Le nozze di Figaro* which, as I can confidently testify after almost fifty years, I still remember vividly: and remember as having been simply wonderful. Mariano Stabile was the best Figaro I have ever heard, in Salzburg and Milan as well as Glyndebourne; and he was, if anything, even better in Rossini's *Barbiere*. The Countess at Glyndebourne, in that year and later, was the Finnish singer, Aulikki Rautawaara. The conductor and director were then, and for many excellent years, Fritz Busch and Carl Ebert. Busch was the equal of, and at times superior to, even Franz Schalk and Bruno Walter; and the Glyndebourne orchestra under him rose to unexpected heights. Ebert must have been the best director of classical opera in Europe. Both were, as is not always the case with even the most gifted artists, men of inborn aesthetic sense and taste; and no composer requires this as much as Mozart. The orchestra was far less accomplished than the Vienna Philharmonic, yet the freshness, the wit, the sheer verve, the inner pulse, the forward movement, the marvellous enthusiasm, lifted it above any performance of *Figaro* I had heard in Salzburg, Munich or anywhere else.

Lotte Lehmann in Salzburg was incomparably the best Countess that I or any member of my generation could have heard; but both the Count (Brownlee) and Figaro (Stabile) acted and sang better at Glyndebourne; Cherubino (Helletsgruber) and Susanna (Mildmay) both sang exquisitely. Not only the gardens, the flowers, the summer evening, the novelty of it all, but that something so enchanted could happen in England at all, that was to me – and surely to many others – a source of lasting astonishment and delight.

There were, of course, the Covent Garden summer seasons, with international casts, often marvellous. But a festival devoted to a particular composer or particular type of opera is something very different. A combination of a great many factors is needed to constitute a festival of the first order. There is the pattern formed by the relationships of the works performed; there is the central conception, the precise direction of the imagination, the

Mozart at Glyndebourne half a century ago

care and unrelenting concentration, which generate a
particular style; there the genuine love of music and
responsiveness of the audiences; above all, the quality of
ensemble, the depth of inner understanding which, for
example, players of chamber music can achieve at their
best: a coherent vision which singers and players can
attain, but all too seldom do. The ensembles achieved at
Glyndebourne were, and are, of unique quality, found,
so far as I can tell, nowhere else.

The right combination of these elements can be
reached momentarily even under repertory conditions:
but continuously only where long preparation and
patient genius are at work. Busch and Ebert created
ensembles which approached perfection. This was made
possible at Glyndebourne where the entire company
lived together for many weeks – their lives and artistic
work became interwoven with one another's during the
late spring and early summer months, so that even those
of moderate gifts were inspired to rise above themselves.
The guidance of the two great masters filled the
musicians with sufficient confidence in their own powers
to achieve a degree of understanding that enabled them
to create their own unique version of the great Mozart
operas. The working conditions at Glyndebourne were
and are unique. Who, in their senses, could have
predicted then with confidence that in an England not
notably devoted to opera in general, or Mozart in
particular, such a venture could be successful? So
brilliantly successful almost immediately after the first
few performances?

As everyone knows, this would not have happened
without the peerless personality of John Christie. He had
the single-mindedness of a secular visionary; he swept
aside objections and apparently insuperable difficulties
pointed out to him by cautious advisers. His boldness,
indomitable will and total independence – above all this

103

last attribute, more often found in England fifty years ago than it is today (for reasons on which I will not speculate) were a major cultural asset to our country. Like every great Intendant in the history of opera, he displayed a degree of personal authority, indeed, of the indispensable element of *terribilità*, which rivalled that of Diaghilev and Toscanini.

It was easier, after all, to create the Salzburg Festival – music in general and opera in particular had been for many years an intrinsic part of Austrian culture and life. Opera in this sense, despite the international seasons at Covent Garden, was not part of the British cultural heritage. John Christie intuitively understood how to realise his ideal, more, I suspect, by instinct and temperament than by rational calculation – the mere appointment of Busch and Ebert was an inspired decision.

Neither of these great masters was a pioneer of methods of interpretation of classical works. Both, I believe, took it for granted that no matter how closely a musical score was related to every nuance of the words or the story, it and it alone played the dominant role: *prima la musica*. The essence of the drama was conveyed by the music. It followed that what mattered above all else was the quality of the singers, the orchestra, the conductor and the chorus master.

After the revolution brought about by Wagner and the conception of the Gesamtkunstwerk, production and design in opera were intended, above all, to serve the music and the words: this alone required the producer, in particular, to be profoundly musical. The libretti might carry clear moral or social or political implications, like those of, for example, *Figaro* or *Fidelio*; but this was not, in the days of which I am writing, as yet generally thought to require additional underlining by the production or the décor: it was assumed that the words and music carried their own overt meaning, given them consciously by their creators; all this set limits to the freedom of expression of performers and producers alike.

Even after the rise of the modern movement in poetry and the visual arts, and even the bold new stage productions of Meyerhold in Moscow and Piscator in Berlin in the 1920s, relatively little attempt was made to bring out by extra-musical means the 'inner' political, sociological, or psycho-pathological significance of libretti and the scores of which the composer and poet showed no conscious awareness. The political import of, say, *Figaro* was, no doubt, clear enough to Mozart and Da Ponte, and certainly to Beaumarchais and the Imperial censors, that of *Rigoletto* and *Don Carlos* to Victor Hugo and Schiller, as well as to Verdi and probably his librettists. But there is, so far as I know, no evidence that – even if any of these artists suspected that their creative imagination might be affected by subliminal forces – they were the unconscious vehicles which carried psychological or sociological content very different from their own conscious conceptions and purposes – that they wished these latent structures or drives to be revealed by the type of techniques later employed by symbolists, expressionists, surrealists, dialectical materialists and the like. Whatever the value of this kind of approach to art in general and opera in particular – and its interest and originality cannot be denied – it is the product of our own day. Neither the composers nor the librettists of the golden age of European opera, from Gluck to the First World War, so far as I know, thought in this fashion; nor did their most admired interpreters before and during the inter-war years. Neither Fritz Busch nor Bruno Walter, neither Arturo Toscanini nor Erich Kleiber, supposed that they were engaged on a task of exhumation, of attempting to breathe a kind of new life – sometimes drawn from the world of the unconscious, individual or collective – into what might otherwise remain noble corpses, museum pieces of little contemporary significance. The masterpieces of both the past and the present spoke to them directly, without reference to processes unknown to their creators, and they, and their producers and designers so conveyed them.

This, too, has in general been the practice of their most gifted successors – we have not been lacking in conductors of genius in our own day. I wish to offer no judgments on the explicit value of these wide differences of approach. The new conception of the immense importance of the producer and the designer, as called upon to lay bare non-rational processes in the minds of the librettist and the composer and their personal or social roots, can be fascinating, and in the hands of musically gifted producers has been sociologically and aesthetically revealing and transforming; and this effect may well be permanent. I wish to do no more than point to the difference between this attitude and the ideals of the founders of Glyndebourne, which seem to me to have given life and sustenance for half a century to this nobly conceived and entirely delightful institution. Long may it flourish.

In 1936 all five of Mozart's most celebrated operas were performed at Glyndebourne. Few who heard Alexander Kipnis (identified correctly, but oddly, as American) as Sarastro in *Die Zauberflöte* are likely to forget it; nor Salvatore Baccaloni as Osmin, nor Julia Moor as Constanze in *Die Entführung*. Moreover, wonder of wonders, it presently became clear that good British singers existed: excellent artists such as Roy Henderson or David Franklin, who, provided they were given adequate conditions, could hold their own in the company of celebrated foreign virtuosi.

Of course the charm and beauty of the Sussex countryside, the divine nature of the music, the technical perfection and exceptional artistic quality of the performances, and year after year the undiminished sense of occasion, all played their part in creating the idyll. For such it was for me and, I wish to believe, for most of the audience at Glyndebourne. But there was also something else: the spontaneity, informality, lack of solemnity of the atmosphere, the total absence of the kind of pomp and circumstance which were such an inevitable (and to their audiences to some extent welcome) attribute of Salzburg and, more particularly, Bayreuth: the sense of continuous enjoyment pervaded everything. All this was, without question, principally due to the personality and clearly felt dictatorship – unpredictable, benevolent, idiosyncratic, generous, life-giving – of one man.

I well remember, both before and after the war, the wonderful spectacle of John Christie, vaguely John Bull-like, perhaps more Churchillian, standing in front of his opera house, at the point at which the cars and buses discharge their loads of visitors, waving them on with impatient gestures into the open doors of the building, much as he must once have marshalled boys at Eton during his career as a master in that establishment. His presence – despite the motley international amalgam of artists, visitors, critics – made the scene utterly and indescribably English, not British but English.

I recall a most exhilarating *Don Pasquale* and a good, but not exceptional, *Macbeth*. But my predominant memories of Glyndebourne before the war are, naturally enough, of Mozart. I have mentioned excellent British singers. Among the masters from abroad, no one who heard Willi Domgraf-Fassbänder as Figaro, Guglielmo, Papageno; Irene Eisinger as Despina, Blondchen, Barbarina; Luise Helletsgruber as Elvira, Dorabella, Cherubino; Salvatore Baccaloni as Leporello; Stabile and Baccaloni as Figaro and Bartolo, or as Malatesta and Don

Pasquale; Walther Ludwig as Belmonte, could possibly ask for a higher degree of musical pleasure, short-lived but intense.

When the young and the middle-aged say, as they often do, that it is a common illusion of the old that there were better singers and performances in the days of their youth, this is not always so: gramophone records (and even some memories) do not delude. The recorded ensembles towards the end of the second act of *Figaro*, in the scene of parting in the first act of *Così*, or the unmasking of Leporello in *Don Giovanni*, are there to testify to the reliability of our memories.

Glyndebourne spread its wings far more widely after the war – *Fidelio*, the brilliant succession of Rossini comedies conducted by Vittorio Gui – a repertoire which outdid the Piccola Scala – the operas of Richard Strauss, Britten, Stravinsky, Donizetti, Bellini, Henze, Monteverdi, Cavalli, Prokofiev, Janáček – the mounting of these with varying, but often splendid, results, is a source of justified pride on the part of the house.

But it is, in the end, its first love – the operas of Mozart – which has continued at the heart of the enterprise. Of course Munich, Vienna, Covent Garden have served Mozart nobly, and above all Salzburg, then and now. But I wish to testify that for me, and I believe I speak for a good many of us in this country, the idea of what an opera by Mozart is and can be, was altered – indeed, transformed – by Glyndebourne and it alone. For a good many members of my generation it was the performances (and, perhaps, at least as much the magnificent recordings, technically imperfect as they must now seem) that shaped our outlook, and vastly raised the ceiling of our expectations. I cannot help rehearsing the sacred litany again – Willi Domgraf-Fassbänder and (the now almost forgotten) Aulikki Rautawaara, John Brownlee and Ivar Andresen, Mariano Stabile and

Salvatore Baccaloni, Irene Eisinger, Audrey Mildmay and Luise Helletsgruber – even the mysterious Sinaida Lissitchkina (over-correctly but uninformatively identified as Nicaraguan) as Queen of the Night – and above all, the matchless ensembles which only Glyndebourne seemed (and still seems) able to generate.

All this became for us the original ideal, the Platonic Idea, imprinted for life on our memory and imagination, no matter how much overlaid and transformed by later experiences, of what the canonical operas by Mozart (including *Idomeneo*) are and remain. It may be that I speak for myself alone. I am reluctant to believe this, but even if it is so, I can only say that in that dawn it was bliss (musically, not at all socially or politically) to be alive.

'An Unexpected Triumph'

Glyndebourne in its Social Setting

Asa Briggs

A visit to Glyndebourne is a unique individual experience. Yet this has seldom stood in the way of massive generalisation about Glyndebourne as an institution and its social as well as its cultural significance. The generalising has ranged from Press comment – as much about the audience as the performance and about the setting as much as the theatre – to sophisticated comparisons between the Glyndebourne Festival and festivals in other countries.

Much of the generalising, however, has been about the role of opera within the British context, and it is fair to add that it is not only 'outsiders' who have indulged in it. The founder of Glyndebourne, John Christie, described by Wilfrid Blunt in his biography, gave a good lead: his programme notes, public speeches and letters to the Press are an indispensable source for the sociologist as well as for the biographer or the historian. It was characteristic of Christie's approach – which he would have hated to have described as sociological – that when in 1959, on the twenty-fifth anniversary of the founding of Glyndebourne, he mounted the stage to present Carl Ebert (his retiring artistic director) with a silver rose-bowl, he spoke for twenty-five minutes, exactly the right length for the occasion, without mentioning either Ebert or the rose-bowl. Covent Garden and the Arts Council figured prominently in the speech, as they have done in much of the other generalising.

It was Christie's remarkable deeds rather than his words which have lived, however, while the words of critics have usually faded into the night. Yet one early critic, Francis Toye of the late *Morning Post*, recognised from the start that great deeds were possible. Christie might lack certain kinds of 'practical wisdom', but he already possessed qualities which could not be taught – 'enthusiasm, unflagging energy and unbounded optimism. Such qualities have enabled men to win unexpected triumphs over seemingly insuperable objects.' Another writer in the *Evening News* was to go further and suggest that Glyndebourne 'will probably live to be an institution'.

Glyndebourne, none the less, was to be a largely unexpected triumph – unexpected by most critics because they shared Christie's own view, still expressed in 1957 in the opening sentence of his Foreword to the Festival Programme, that 'Britain has been an unoperatic country', or, as he put it more generally in a letter of 1943 to the BBC, 'England is musically an underbred country'. One of his very first articles on his 'Glyndebourne project', which appeared in the *Monthly Musical Record* in 1933, began with the generalisation, 'Part of the public [in England] does not clamour for opera because it has not been well impressed, another part because it chooses as long as it can to remain ignorant, while the enthusiast, owing to the low England standard, goes abroad.' If the middle phrase 'chooses . . . to remain ignorant' begs more questions than it answers, the phrases about the first and second sections of the public were obvious and familiar enough to all observers of music in Britain, not to speak of participants in music-making. It was obvious and familiar, too, that the size of the first group was far greater than the third, and that it could be equally articulate.

Partly through what Glyndebourne has offered – opera of an unprecedented standard in England in a superb English setting – the size of the first group has been reduced, and the activities of the third have been transformed. 'Enthusiasts' still rightly go abroad, but they have to go to Glyndebourne too, and while there remains a public outside which, for whatever reasons, is ignorant of opera, it flaunts its ignorance less securely than it used to do. W. J. Turner, writing in *Music and Letters* in 1934 of the first performance of *Così fan tutte*, remarked that he personally would like to have excluded from the performance many of the people he saw there. They were philistines, but they belonged 'to no one class, stratum, occupation or profession'. He stopped at that point because, he said, of the law of libel.

Other less musical critics placed more emphasis on class. From the start, a vocal section of the popular press dismissed the Glyndebourne audience as 'snobs', focusing more on the champagne they drank in the garden or the wines in the restaurant than on the music they listened to in the theatre. Yet while such critics pointed to such specific Glyndebourne social features as wearing evening dress in the daytime – and Carl Ebert himself could refer to *Die Snobs* – they were usually at the same time criticising British opera audiences as a whole. They deemed opera to be not only a minority but a highbrow taste, a 'foreign interest', which particularly appealed to the rich – and to the titled, not all of whom were rich – and for that reason to the 'snobs'. Opera was usually associated, therefore, not with society with a small s, but with Society with a large S, and often not with culture with a small c but with Kultur with a capital K. It was 'U', though the U/non-U distinction had not yet been devised. It attracted fashion critics as well as music critics, and Glyndebourne in particular was almost always news in the gossip columns. Indeed, these, with all their limitations, remain one of the best sources for the social historian, for no one bothered to collect any details of the social composition of opera audiences in Britain until the 1960s – and such details are still sparse.

From limited evidence available, it is clear that Glyndebourne from the start had a broader audience than the critics suggested and that it broadened it further as its reputation grew. It included 'locals' from Ringmer, Lewes and the surrounding area, not least Brighton; businessmen and their employees, mainly from London, lured there for a variety of motives, but with some of them visiting opera for the first time; and finally Turner's musical enthusiasts, among them some, at least, of his fellow music critics. By the late 1960s, when the Arts Council produced a report on opera and ballet, it could be claimed more generally that 'opera as an art form not only continues to attract the leading composers of the day, but is also attracting a growing audience drawn from a cross-section of the community, with an accent towards youth'.

The specific contribution of Glyndebourne to the process of change was made, as a result of efficient financing in often difficult and unprecedented circumstances – largely independent financing. Opera cannot rest on box office receipts alone. It requires patrons or sponsors or subsidies. By its nature it is not cheap. Nor are its costs easy to control. It is against the economic odds, therefore, that the process of social and cultural change has advanced. And sociologists often overlook the economics. Carl Ebert, Fritz Busch and Rudolf Bing, when they joined Christie at Glyndebourne, all came to Britain as refugees from a German-Austrian background, where private and public patronage of opera was taken for granted: they had been involved also in the management, musical and organisational, of opera houses. There was no such tradition in Britain, national or local, although by 1957 Britain was offering public subsidies for opera to the extent of £400,000 a year, small subsidies by German or Italian standards, but in themselves significant evidence of a change of attitudes.

Glyndebourne was outside the subsidies, but this important fact concerned Christie less than the fact that the change which had taken place seemed to him to be the result of what was obviously a healthy enthusiasm rather than the triumph of organisation. 'Obviously this should have been planned as a whole, but it has not been planned.' The corollary was plain for Christie. 'So Glyndebourne must step in and put forward its scheme' for opera in the future. The Foreword of 1957 states somewhat vaguely what Christie then had in mind – although there was no vagueness in his sentence, 'The music decides it all.' He wanted Britain to evolve its own approach to the organisation of opera. 'What matters is the result. The finance will solve itself. Waste can be cut out ... Examine the history of opera in this country. Don't copy the rest of the world. Fix responsibility on shoulders qualified to bear it. Understand the nature and principles of the problem before us ... Pay only for results. Britain can lead.'

Britain was not to follow Christie's road in 1957, although, as the Arts Council Report noted, the size of the opera audience has greatly increased since then and its composition and habits have changed. The number of young people in the audience has grown. And the growth of provincial opera companies and of amateur as well as professional activity – themselves a by-product of the

development of the educational system – have stimu-
lated a more knowledgeable enthusiasm. Meanwhile,
Glyndebourne, which has benefited from such social
and cultural change, has remained as independent in
its organisation, operations and policies as it was in
Christie's mind. Its distinctiveness has been its strength,
and it might have lost it had it been integrated into a
bigger plan, even a plan of his choosing. It is interesting
to note, therefore, that one aspect of its distinctiveness
which meant much to Christie himself, namely its
unique physical setting, did not figure in the original
Monthly Musical Record article of 1933. Christie discussed
his hopes for Glyndebourne without once mentioning
the special feature of Glyndebourne which has always
attracted audiences and which has accounted in part for
the sense of an individual experience, even for people
who know little of opera.

In his book on his world tour of festivals, *Conducted
Tour*, Bernard Levin in 1982 was to call his chapter on
Glyndebourne 'The Enchanted Garden'. It was a more
vivid phrase than the pastoral English of the first
published prospectus of 1934, which referred to an
'ancient Tudor Manor House' set in 'a beautiful wooded
stretch of the Sussex Downs' and described how 'within
a quarter-of-an-hour's stroll of the house is a chain of
woodland pools following the course of a Downland
stream, leading to coppices carpeted with wild flowers.'
Garden flowers have been more a feature of the appeal of
Glyndebourne than wild flowers, Art as much as Nature,
not least in the long picnic intervals; and on the occasion
in 1959 of the twenty-fifth anniversary of Glyndebourne,
John Christie was to mention 'Harvey (the head gar-
dener) in control of the gardens, where all work in
complete happiness', and to include a photograph of him
in the Programme.

In his first article of 1933, however, Christie had

concentrated properly not on the natural setting, but on the musical and social setting. 'The Glyndebourne Opera House,' he explained, 'has two possibilities:

(1)   to offer superb performances to people who will regard them as the chief thing in the day or week to be looked forward to, and who will not try to sandwich them between business interviews and a society party;
(2)   to give educational performances for the ordinary public, with the best possible stage setting and only English orchestras and lesser known singers.'

'I incline towards the superb performance,' he went on, 'assisted by a marvellous holiday *Festspiel* atmosphere, but expense would prevent the admission of the poorer part of the public, and so it may be desirable to give local performances after the *Festspiel* is over. We also hope to have Shakespeare festivals and fairly frequent concerts. At all performances the feeling of general happiness and benevolence should be conspicuous. The scenery and lighting, being designed new for every opera, should be superb. There are no vested interests, no traditions in the way.'

It was a powerful manifesto, which did not attempt to deny that there were choices. Neither did John Christie suggest that his delightful phrase, 'general happiness and benevolence' (compare the happiness of the gardeners), could be translated into Jeremy Bentham's language of 'the greatest happiness of the greatest number'. What does stand out – and Glyndebourne was always to endeavour to live up to it – was a non-Benthamite emphasis on quality, on 'superb performance', visual as well as musical. A similar inclination was to move the first designers of the BBC's new Third Programme after the end of the Second World War, when they faced up to the same choices and rejected a specifically educational mission in favour of delight (while not seeking to deny that education in the arts was possible and that many of the people who were ignorant were not ignorant through their own choice). 'We hope that our audience will enjoy itself without crutches' and that it will include 'the most intelligent, receptive people in all classes, persons who value artistic experience all the more because of the limited opportunities they have of enjoying it.'

Christie would have liked the BBC to have been integrated into his 'plan' for opera in 1957. 'I take the view,' he had written in June 1946 to Sir William Haley, then the Director-General of the BBC and a dedicated believer in the Third Programme, 'that the BBC has got to take a hand in helping England to get the right performances, in finding or achieving the right artists and in getting the right organisations at work to achieve these two purposes.' He was unhappy at that time even about narrower considerations within its remit – the fees paid to Glyndebourne for broadcast performances, for example – but he always had an eye on a more general strategy of advance. Rudolf Bing, then his general manager, had directly related fees paid in 1946 to the buying of a Glyndebourne package. 'We cannot see at all,' he wrote to the Outside Broadcasting Manager of the BBC, 'why a fee paid by the BBC should merely cover the actual cost which is caused to the promoter by a broadcast, e.g. fees to the artists and musicians etc. A broadcast of a Glyndebourne performance contains, in our view, a considerable amount of goodwill which Glyndebourne has built up and paid for.' And Bing had at least one influential supporter in the BBC, George (later Sir George) Barnes, who was to become first Director of Television. He was then in charge of the Third Programme and wrote to Haley in August 1946, 'I cannot stress too strongly the importance to the Third Programme of successful negotiations with Glyndebourne. For us to miss in the first year of our existence ... Glyndebourne 1947 would, in my opinion, be a catastrophe.'

By then, Glyndebourne counted for the BBC as much as Covent Garden. Yet between then and 1957 it had begun a reorganisation of its finances which transformed its structure while maintaining its atmosphere, the second of its unexpected triumphs; and, having outlasted the *Morning Post*, it was now to outlast the Third Programme. By 1939, when the Festival made a small surplus following its sixth and longest season, John Christie had spent over £100,000 of his own money on the venture, but he found it very difficult to cope with its restoration in 1945 after the interval of the war, a very different kind of break from the long Glyndebourne intervals. It was during the early part of this interval, during the phoney war, that Christie wrote to F.W. Ogilvie, then Director-General of the BBC, expressing the hope that Glyndebourne would receive 'a fair consideration in the future'. 'I know that it is easy,' Christie explained to Ogilvie, 'though entirely untrue, to suggest that Glyndebourne is for the rich. Most of our patrons make some sacrifice of something else in order to get there ... I have managed to keep afloat, but at the expense of doing new works.'

How much more difficult the position was in 1946 was made clear in Christie's letter to the then Director-General of the BBC, Haley. 'We are faced with the problem of restoring Glyndebourne in spite of every conceivable obstruction and difficulty and of obviously increased costs. After seven years the apparatus has all to be overhauled, taken down, restored and replaced ... We have undertaken to restart Glyndebourne with our own resources this year and next. How much is involved financially we cannot yet tell ... We are constituted not for profit. There is a heavy debt from the past in which

we are involved.' Yet there was a comparative opportunity too, for as Christie was to write in retrospect in
1954 the War had left many of the leading opera houses
smashed in Germany and Austria. 'The French are not
very intrusive in opera. [A characteristic Christie statement.] The three British opera houses were untouched.
There is little opera in the United States. Here is
Britain's opportunity.'

By 1946, the Arts Council, a body corporate, was on
the scene beside the BBC and there was also a Minister
for the Arts for the first time, although the status (and
qualifications for the post) have varied considerably
between 1946 and the present. The emergence of a new
institution was evidence of what an American scholar,
Janet Minihan, in a pioneering study has called the
'nationalisation of culture' – and the BBC had certainly
contributed to that. Yet while the Council was to support
opera and ballet out of its limited funds, Glyndebourne
was not a beneficiary. Few people saw the opportunity of
such 'nationalisation' as clearly as Christie, and yet his
relations with Lord Keynes, his powerful neighbour in
Sussex, who had much to do with the creation of the
Council and was also first Chairman of the post-war
Covent Garden Opera Trust, were strained; and it was
not until the Glyndebourne Touring Company came into
existence in 1968 that any Arts Council funds made their
way annually to Glyndebourne. It is important to note
that when they came then, this was not so much
evidence of the 'nationalisation of culture' or of an
attempt to place Britain in an international league, as of
the desire of the Council to diffuse 'culture' in the
provinces and to stimulate provincial as distinct from
metropolitan performances.

Despite all Christie's pleas, therefore, Glyndebourne
after 1946 had to stand on its own feet just as it had had
to learn very quickly to stand on its own feet in the first

exciting days of the Christie family venture. The first casualty was Rudolf Bing, an impresario before he came to Britain, who feared that neither adequate State support nor private support would be forthcoming in the difficult post-war years, and for this and other reasons resigned the general managership of Glyndebourne in 1948, becoming general manager of the Metropolitan Opera House, New York, in the autumn of the following year. This, a colleague told him was 'a dazzling opportunity, you are right in accepting'. His successor, Moran Caplat, was to find opportunity at Glyndebourne and to remain in his post for the next thirty-one years, during which Glyndebourne completely re-established itself as an institution and on different lines economically from those before 1939. If the key to its successful finance was, as always, the raising of enough income from sources other than box office receipts – and these depended on the length of season and the number, range and prices of seats – in order to cover the costs of producing an attractive Glyndebourne programme, it was forced to re-think its position not once but many times.

The method eventually discovered, pragmatically rather than through imitation of other models, was characteristically British, step-by-step and piece-by-piece. There was to be a variety of sources and a variety of opportunities for private funds. Moreover, the first new idea – that of the Glyndebourne Festival Society set up in 1951 – was more like that of a British football supporters' club than German or Italian musical patronage. John Christie's 'privileged guests' of pre-war days were to rally round the Glyndebourne venture when it most needed them. And 'the snobs' were to turn out to be the committed enthusiasts. 'What the audience at Glyndebourne may eventually be and do,' the *Observer* had written in June 1934, 'it is impossible to say.' Now in

1951 it had become possible, for it was they first and foremost who had to rally round. While politicians and civil servants were always prominent among the Glyndebourne audience – and still are – there was only one year, 1951, when Glyndebourne received a Treasury grant for its main base activities. As a reward for its contribution – an all Mozart Festival – to the Festival of Britain it received a £25,000 guarantee against loss. With the passage of time, the independence conferred by absence of public funding came to be regarded as a unique asset, though Arts Council grants to the Touring Opera, which made its first provincial tour in 1968, were greatly welcomed and keenly fought for when they seemed to be in jeopardy. It had to be emphasised then – as it has to be emphasised now – that without Glyndebourne Festival, there could have been no Glyndebourne Touring.

There was an element not so much of 'unexpected success' as of hard-won success in the achievement of financial independence, and it came from a distinctive combination of individual and corporate support. A family venture became a broader team-venture without the sense of family ever being lost. Indeed, the first corporate support had a family dimension to it. John Spedan Lewis of the John Lewis Partnership, who before the war had given his employees, John Lewis 'partners', £2 tickets for Glyndebourne when they were due for a bonus, came to 'the rescue of Glyndebourne' (in Christie's words) and guaranteed £12,000 to underwrite two operas in 1950. When in 1951 another earlier Glyndebourne benefactor, Miki Sekers of the West Cumberland Silk Mills, suggested the idea of the Glyndebourne Festival Society and, as part of its function, a suitable and effective way of raising corporate finance would be through advertisement in a handsome annual programme – forty advertisers, he suggested, would bring in £20,000 gross – the John Lewis Partnership was among the first eighteen. That year the Glyndebourne Festival Society was set up and O.B. (later Sir Bernard) Miller, who was to be Chairman of the Partnership, was a member (and, after 1965, Chairman) of the Glyndebourne Festival Society Committee.

The first prospectus of the Glyndebourne Festival Society, published in December 1951, laid down as the main objective the raising of £25,000 a year to cover the difference between the cost of running the Festival and box office receipts. There were to be three kinds of membership: individual, associated and corporate. Individual members were to pay an annual subscription of £26 11s., entitling them to two free seats and a free copy of the new Festival Programme; associated members were to pay an annual subscription of £2 2s., entitling them to a free programme only; and corporate members were to pay £105, entitling them to four free seats a season.

The response to the prospectus was enthusiastic – and immediate. By the time the 1952 season opened, the new Society had no fewer than 806 members, 25 of them corporate, 65 individual and 716 associate. Yet given new income from the Society and the programme book, there was still a deficit of £17,790 on the 1952 season. It was against this background that it was decided to run the Festival Opera through a Trust, an idea originally conceived by John Christie during the war. The idea was perfected over tea at Glyndebourne, in February 1953, and the Trust formally came into existence in May 1954. The Trust was to work with a new company to be called Glyndebourne Productions Ltd, which was to plan the artistic and financial details of the season and submit its budget to the Trust. The Trust, to whom the house, theatre and gardens at Glyndebourne were conveyed on a long lease at a peppercorn rent, was in future 'to be

responsible for the general supervision of these proper-
ties and of the Glyndebourne Festival Opera.' However
there was always a very close relationship between
family and Trust and between the sense of money and
the sound of music.

In the longer run, the further broadening of the
national opera audience was to depend on the interest in
opera taken by the media, including the recording
companies, and the role of the BBC was to be crucial.
Yet it was not to have a monopoly. The first televised
BBC opera from Glyndebourne, *Così*, had been broadcast in 1951. In 1972 Southern Television began a series
of widely appreciated transmissions of Glyndebourne
operas in full. The relationship between Glyndebourne
audiences on the spot and the distant audiences scattered in their homes is obviously difficult to analyse.
Stage and screen set quite different conditions, at least
of reception and production. So, too, do auditorium and
armchairs. Yet numbers always dazzle, and Lionel
Salter, then Head of Music Productions at BBC Television, made much of the point in *Opera* (November
1957) that 'the number of people who watched the
Glyndebourne relay of Rossini's *Le Comte Ory* would be
equivalent to full houses at Glyndebourne every single
night throughout the year, Sundays included, for *fifteen
years*.'

Although there might have been viewers who preferred *La Bohème* without the background music – a point
once made by Barnes – Salter suggested that what had
been taken to be an English prejudice against opera was
'only a matter of opportunity and familiarity'; and one of
his BBC colleagues, Kenneth Wright, pointed out more
than once that 'opera, the most complicated and prob-
lematic of all musical art forms', had none the less 'given
us many of the great masterpieces in the whole literature
of music, and moreover a galaxy of tunes so good and so

lovable that they are known and whistled by round heads, long heads, flat heads and even artistic fat heads all the world over.' While Glyndebourne audiences remained severely restricted in size despite an expansion of the theatre – and there was usually a scramble for seats – the BBC (and Southern Television later) were thinking in terms not so much of that minority but of course of a mass audience: in Wright's phrase, 'the task of bringing opera to the millions'.

The recording companies have to be brought in also because, as H.G. Pollard – writing in *The Gramophone* in March 1952 – put it, 'a good modern record, when played by equipment of the first quality, can create an illusion of actuality of musical performance that no wireless broadcast can achieve under the limitations of present-day broadcasting.' Pollard was accused of exaggeration, but recording has made enormous strides since then, and video recording has opened up the possibilities of individual choice of operas in the home. Glyndebourne has played an important part in this story, and intends to play a more important part still in the future.

Yet, however important the cultural role of the media, the financial underpinning of Glyndebourne as a Festival remained dependent on business. After 1952 there was to develop a fourfold business interest in Glyndebourne. First, the number of corporate members of the Society – 'firms and industrial institutions' – increased; second, so also did the number of advertisers in the programmes – by 1964 there were 39, still one short of Seker's original target figure; third, sponsorship of particular operas was sought after. The first such sponsorship was that of the Peter Stuyvesant Foundation, which in 1966 provided a grant of £35,000 over seven years to sponsor the staging of new productions, the first being *Don Giovanni* in 1967 (the next new production of which ten years later was to be financed by Imperial Tobacco); and fourth, funds

20 Nicholas Maw's *The Rising of the Moon*, a Glyndebourne commission. Richard Van Allan with Anne Howells

21 Kiri Te Kanawa as the Countess, with Benjamin Luxon as the Count, in the 1973 *Figaro*

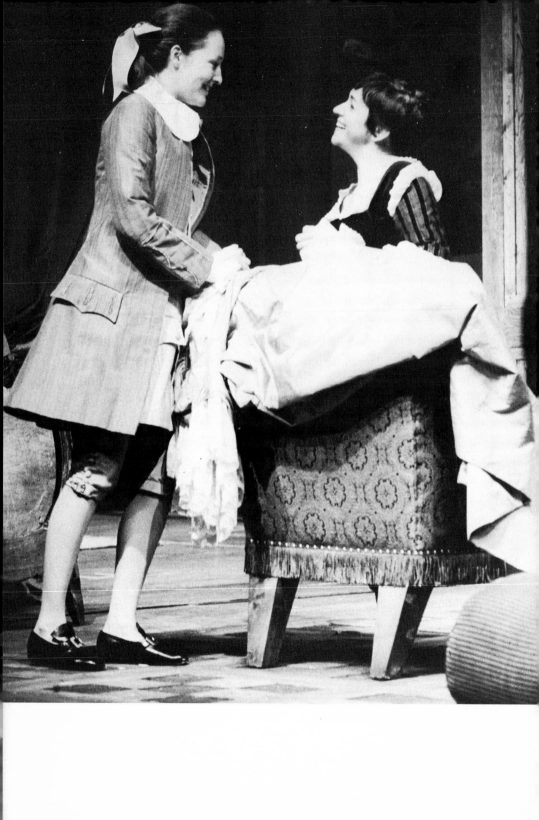

22, 23, 24 and 25   Some of Glyndebourne's favourite ladies. *Facing page*, Frederica von Stade and Ileana Cotrubas in *Figaro* (1973); *above*, Elisabeth Söderström, with Marco Bakker, in *Intermezzo* (1974); *below left*, Janet Baker in *Orfeo ed Euridice* (1982); *below right*, Maria Ewing as Rosina, with John Rawnsley as Figaro in *Barbiere* (1982)

26   John Pritchard in rehearsal
27   The management at Glyndebourne, October 1983. *At the back, left*, George Christie, *right* Peter Hall, *and seated, left*, Brian Dickie, *right* Bernard Haitink
28   David Hockney and John Cox (*right*) discuss the set for *The Rake's Progress*

were provided for specialised Glyndebourne ventures, notably a Chorus Scheme, which started in 1976 followed by the Musical Preparation Scheme in 1981, and a Building Fund which was set up in 1982.

This neat list suggests simplicity of design. In fact, there was a major change in fund-raising methods at Glyndebourne, guided to an important extent by Sir Alex Alexander, who became a Trustee of Glyndebourne in 1975 at a time when he was Chairman of Imperial Food. Policy before the mid-1970s had been to rely on box office receipts to cover 80 per cent of costs. There were, however, warning signs in the early 1970s which became more insistent in subsequent years, and by 1975, in a period of steep inflation (and economic disturbance), it became clear that box office revenue could not keep pace with costs – a problem faced by every opera house in the West at that time. Accordingly dependence on the box office dropped to something a little under 70 per cent of expenditure.

Against this background the Finance Committee, a subsidiary to the Arts Trust, was set up in 1975 to tap alternative sources of finance. It had to seek support for various objects, as listed above, and it showed great ingenuity in doing so. Indeed, if the Festival Society saved Glyndebourne in 1951, this action on the part of the Trustees – and of the Finance Committee in particular – saved it in 1975.

In 1962 George Christie wrote that Glyndebourne presented annual seasons which were 'full-up' months before they began and that it had 'naturally enough come to be regarded as part of the established order of events in this country.' Indeed, T.S. Eliot might well have included it in a later version of the list of such events which he set out in 1947 in his *Notes Towards a Definition of Culture*, along with Wimbledon, Henley, Derby Day and the Cup Final. George Christie feared that in future

Glyndebourne: A Celebration

Glyndebourne might be tempted to sit back on a cushion of unexpected success, more hazardous than 'the mysterious and unexpected success' of its early years. In fact, any such fears have been unjustified. The only cushions are at picnics in the garden. Glyndebourne is, and will be.

A Foreigner at Glyndebourne

Bernard Haitink

It is just as dangerous to have a reputation for being a 'concert conductor' as it is to be considered an opera specialist. Even the word 'conductor' is misleading. To be a musician is the most important thing. I felt very imprisoned to be labelled a concert conductor. I was, to start with, in a peculiar position in Holland, because I had always wanted to be involved in opera; but it is a country with a tremendous tradition for concert work – with the Concertgebouw as the standard-bearer. The three conductors in charge of that orchestra had been Kes, Mengelberg and van Beinum, none of whom had been very keen on the theatre. Mengelberg was with the orchestra for fifty years and the nearest he got to opera was with Mendelssohn's incidental music for *A Midsummer Night's Dream*.

As a young man I felt very worried about the absence of any opera in my career in Holland. At this stage I was thrown into the icy waters of the Concertgebouw, far too young and with all the members of the orchestra older than I was. They seemed to me arrogant and conceited and not as good as they thought they were. I therefore had to battle to survive and there was scarcely any chance at that time to think about opera, except for three occasions which I look back on with misgivings: *Don Giovanni*, *Don Carlos* and *Der fliegende Holländer*. With hindsight I see that Dutch opera was not flourishing in Holland at that time and so did not provide me with the context I needed.

I cannot survive in opera if the team is not right – and opera depends on a team. I function when I know that I am surrounded by people who can pave the way but not shield me, who can provide motivation, bringing out the best of my talent.

My contact in England started with the Hallé Orchestra. I then came to London to the London Philharmonic Orchestra and felt that I had something to say to them. All of a sudden I became the orchestra's principal conductor. Some people in Holland didn't like this as they felt they owned me and I belonged to Holland. However, the London period gave me a lot of satisfaction artistically and helped considerably in developing my musical authority.

Then the Glyndebourne proposal came along. I remember Moran Caplat sitting in a coffee shop in Wigmore Street asking me if I would do *Die Entführung* in 1972. I accepted. I had little idea of the theatre when I conducted that *Entführung*, but Glyndebourne asked me back to do *Die Zauberflöte*. It was an old production and I don't think I added much to that Mozart tradition which is so much part of Glyndebourne.

Glyndebourne was patient. They invited me back to do *The Rake's Progress* and that was the breakthrough. All of a sudden I realised that you can make music in the theatre when things are going right on stage. The inspiration was suddenly there and my theatre instincts at last emerged.

I know, having started as a concert conductor, that one is not fulfilled artistically without the added dimension of the opera house. I want to have experience in both fields. I think no one can fully understand the Mozart symphonies without having conducted his operas. Similarly it helps to gain the full understanding of Bruckner's symphonies to have had experience of conducting Wagner's operas.

In the theatre you are the heartbeat of the performance and that is the feeling you should both give and receive. So much of what is happening in opera focuses the attention on the stage. Whereas the conductor is very visible in the concert hall, often he can barely be seen by the audience in the opera house. Yet I want his presence in the opera house to be as felt as in the concert hall.

The marriage between theatre and the concert hall is invigorating for me. When I have finished at Glyndebourne I dread going back to the concert season, but when I finish the concert season I long to get back to Glyndebourne – despite the fact that my heart is also with such a superb orchestra as the Concertgebouw and with the symphonic world.

Chance might have made me start in another and bigger opera house but I don't think I would have fitted in as well as I have in Glyndebourne. There a marvellous team exists and a marvellous tradition; and it doesn't run all the year round but instead operates on a limited number of productions in a concentrated period. In that context I can flourish and it has turned out to be a very lucky choice.

The highlights for me have been *The Rake's Progress, A Midsummer Night's Dream* and of course my work with Sir Peter Hall on the Mozart operas. What always appealed to me was that Glyndebourne followed lines of thought; first of all Mozart's operas and then the Strauss comedies – as well as the Rossini comedies – and the baroque repertory. We now focus our attention on the start of a new line of thought, which I hope will be the Verdi operas in co-operation with Peter Hall – we shall try to give a fresh approach to these operas in a theatre the size of which is not customarily associated with this part of the operatic repertory.

Glyndebourne's Extensions

Gillian Widdicombe

John Christie always longed to extend his musical empire, especially in the early years when Glyndebourne could seat only 311 people, and a dozen performances seemed enough for Sussex. The auditorium stretched gradually to 830 seats, and the number of performances each season settled at an average of 65 during the 1960s. But John Christie was the first to realise that enlarging the palace would probably defeat the excellence and therefore the object of the empire. Characteristically, his dreams and schemes were far more grandiose and ambitious: he wanted Glyndebourne to have a wide audience and influence outside Sussex.

His unfulfilled dreams even included the staging of a huge production of *Aida* at the Coliseum in 1937; and he nursed the covetous hope that Beecham would make such 'a muddle and a loss' at Covent Garden in 1938 that Glyndebourne would be able to take over the management of that theatre too. Beecham did in fact invite Rudolf Bing (Glyndebourne's general manager from 1936 to 1948) to manage Covent Garden, and Bing's plans progressed as far as preparing to bring two of Ebert's famous large-scale productions to London in 1939: the 1937 production of *Carmen* from Vienna, conducted by Bruno Walter; and the 1932 production of *Un ballo in maschera* from Berlin, conducted by Fritz Busch. Meanwhile, Bing was also busy arranging for Glyndebourne to travel abroad, to the Lucerne Festival and the New York World Fair in 1939.

International affairs defeated all such plans. The notion of Glyndebourne performing outside its home theatre was eventually pursued as an economical solution to the problems created by the Second World War. The notion of regular touring took much longer to give birth; and when it did, with the advent of Glyndebourne Touring Opera in 1968, the motivation was both more adventurous and more modern than anything John Christie had conceived. As for the wider audience and influence: with the hindsight of half a century we may observe that Glyndebourne achieved this, in its early years, through the gramophone, radio and television.

In 1934 not even one of Mozart's operas was available in its entirety on gramophone record in Britain. But the time was ripe, and even before Glyndebourne's modest first season opened with twelve performances divided between *Le nozze di Figaro* and *Così fan tutte*, Fred Gaisberg and David Bicknell of His Master's Voice visited Sussex and expressed interest. They chose *Figaro*, with Willi Domgraf-Fassbänder as Figaro, Audrey Mildmay as Susanna, Roy Henderson as the Count, Aulikki Rautawaara as the Countess, Luise Helletsgruber as Cherubino and Heddle Nash as Basilio. It was all so simple and convenient. HMV's mobile recording van was driven down to Sussex; the singers were lined up at the front of the stage, the orchestra stayed in the pit. All the concerted ensembles were recorded, making six 78rpm discs which were attractively boxed and issued as the first volume of 'The Mozart Opera Society'.* HMV were so pleased with the result that the following season they recorded more (but not quite all) of the rest of that opera, making two more boxes including the overture, most of the solo arias and duets, but not the *secco* recitatives. As William Mann says in *Opera on Record* (Hutchinson, London, 1979):

> In its day the cast was vastly admired; two decades and a bit later, disappointment extended beyond the omissions to the actual singing, most of it dry or inexpert or downright unstylish, Heddle Nash's Basilio an oasis of musicality, even without his aria.

But HMV's second venture was an outstanding and lasting success, for during the same days as they completed *Figaro*, in June 1935, they took what seemed then a considerable plunge: the complete recording of that opera so dear to Glyndebourne, *Così fan tutte*. Nash, Domgraf-Fassbänder and Helletsgruber returned to the microphone for Ferrando, Guglielmo and Dorabella; John Brownlee sang Alfonso and Irene Eisinger a squeaky Despina; but the triumph was the dramatic Fiordiligi of the American-born soprano Ina Souez. The recitatives were also recorded, with Busch accompanying them on the piano (as he resolutely continued to do until his death). Half a century later, reissued on LPs, the technical quality of the sound is remarkably clear, though of course it is boxy; the performance is alive and fluent, and Busch's conducting is still considered revelatory: brisk, firm and sensitive.

In 1936 HMV's mobile van returned yet again during the last week of June to record *Don Giovanni* with an

---

*All the gramophone recordings mentioned in this article are available at the National Sound Archive, London SW7.

equally fine Donna Anna from Souez, Salvatore Baccaloni's delightful Leporello, an aristocratic performance
by John Brownlee of the title role, a girlish Zerlina from
Audrey Mildmay and a boyish Masetto from Roy Henderson. Today these recordings have rightly acquired
legendary status, for they enabled Mozart's three finest
operas to be studied and enjoyed outside the theatre for
the first time; they also provide splendid evidence of
what Glyndebourne was like in its youth. At the time,
however, the only obvious signs of importance were that
Fritz Busch found his reputation abroad much enhanced,
and John Christie began, with pride and joy, to pile
hatboxes full of 78rpm records around the house.

The war disrupted the sequence, and afterwards it was
Decca who seized the chance to record Kathleen Ferrier
in an abridged version of Glyndebourne's 1947 production of Gluck's *Orfeo*. Ferrier's performance matured
dramatically after this recording, and many years later
HMV released a Dutch radio recording of a live performance given with the Netherlands Opera in 1951, which
surpassed Glyndebourne's.

When Busch returned to Glyndebourne in 1950, so
did HMV, for this proved to be one of the vintage
performances of *Così fan tutte*, led by Sena Jurinac as
Fiordiligi and Richard Lewis as Ferrando. Alas, only
excerpts were recorded – for instance, including 'Come
scoglio' but omitting 'Un aura amorosa'; and though
many a critic still chooses Busch, Jurinac and Lewis as
principal ingredients in the perfect cast, this classic
recording has not been reissued recently by HMV.

The year 1951 was a memorable one for Glynde-
bourne. The season opened with the famous production
of *Idomeneo*, with Jurinac as Ilia, Lewis as Idomeneo,
Birgit Nilsson as Electra and Léopold Simoneau as
Idamante; HMV immediately decided to record it.
Unfortunately Busch was taken ill during the season and

Nilsson and Simoneau were unable to sing in the recording; so only excerpts were recorded. Only two weeks later, Busch suddenly died of a heart attack in his London hotel, at the age of 61. HMV subsequently regretted that they had not done *Idomeneo* properly, and in 1952 returned to record Ebert's production complete, again with Jurinac and Lewis, but conducted by John Pritchard (Busch's former assistant). This was an international success, marketed by Seraphim in the USA with extracts from the review which championed it as: 'A splendid keepsake of a production which must surely rank among Glyndebourne's greatest, a noble performance of the work in which Mozart's dramatic genius first attained its full stature.' For more than a dozen years *Idomeneo* received no other recording.

Idomeneo closed two chapters in Glyndebourne's history. It was the last of the Busch-Mozart recordings, and it was the last of the 78rpm records. As new recording techniques requiring studio facilities were developed, Glyndebourne's advantages for recording faded, but the arrival of Vittorio Gui and Rossini's operas rejuvenated HMV's interest. They began with the 1953 production of *La cenerentola*, with Juan Oncina, Marina de Gabarain and the inimitable Sesto Bruscantini; and then there was the delicious 1955 production of *Le Comte Ory*, enchantingly sung by Oncina and Sari Barabas. Rather adventurously, HMV also recorded Pritchard's performance of Busoni's *Arlecchino*, with Geraint Evans and Ian Wallace, but then deleted it almost immediately.

Mozart's impending bicentenary in 1956 inspired HMV to record *Le nozze di Figaro* again, with Jurinac as the Countess and Bruscantini (then her husband) as Figaro. Graziella Sciutti sang Susanna, though she had not yet done so on stage in Sussex; and this crucial substitution proved to be a turning point in Glyndebourne's relationship with the record companies. It was clear that the sort of singers who could be persuaded to sing a dozen performances in Sussex were no longer always those acceptable to an international record company; and when HMV announced its intention to record *Il barbiere di Siviglia* in 1962, it was pleased to have Gui with Alva, Bruscantini and Ian Wallace; but instead of Glyndebourne's Alberta Valentini as Rosina, the recording was made with Victoria de los Angeles, who never set foot in Sussex, but had already recorded a promising performance of this role for Cetra. The result was a sweet, enchanting recording, unrivalled even by Callas or Berganza.

As the star system flourished, Glyndebourne lost touch with the record industry until by reviving the baroque repertoire it gave itself another clear advantage. HMV recorded the 1963 production of *L'incoronazione di Poppea*, with Magda Laszlo, Richard Lewis, and with Hugues Cuénod and Oralia Dominguez leading the character roles. Argo recorded both the Cavalli operas, conducted by Raymond Leppard: *L'Ormindo*, with its large cast including John Wakefield, Hanneke van Bork, Anne Howells, Jane Berbié and Cuénod, in 1969; and *La Calisto* with Janet Baker, Ileana Cotrubas and James Bowman, in 1972. A state of feebleness then overtook the record companies that had for so long been associated with Glyndebourne; and when the Peter Hall production of Monteverdi's *Il ritorno d'Ulisse* proved too good to be missed altogether, it was recorded by CBS, with Glyndebourne's cast led by Frederica von Stade and Richard Stilwell as Penelope and Ulysses. When Dame Janet Baker chose Gluck's *Orfeo ed Euridice* as her farewell to opera at Glyndebourne in 1982, the notable opportunity to record it was taken by Erato. And now in 1984 EMI have returned to the Glyndebourne fold to record *Don Giovanni* with Bernard Haitink conducting and Thomas Allen in the title role.

That the general public felt that the record companies had missed a number of interesting things at Glyndebourne became obvious with the advent of 'pirate' recordings, mostly emanating from the USA, and apparently infringing both Glyndebourne's copyright and that of the BBC. These tend to feature stars who sang at Glyndebourne before their fees started to dazzle. Thus the 1964 production of *Idomeneo* has survived, with Gundula Janowitz as Ilia, Luciano Pavarotti as Idamante, and Lewis singing Idomeneo. The same company has also produced an abridged version of *Der Rosenkavalier* with Montserrat Caballé singing the Marschallin (her British début) in 1965. And for Britten scholars, from another source there is a single disc of excerpts from the unrevised score of *The Rape of Lucretia* with the cast which sang at Glyndebourne in 1946 – an interesting comparison to the revised version officially recorded later for Decca by the Sadler's Wells company.

The BBC has done Glyndebourne loyal and useful service. When Glyndebourne was born, the BBC was only twelve years old, but it had a number of studio opera broadcasts as well as relays to its credit; and even in the 1920s the view was being put forward that the future stability of British opera companies might well depend on indirect subsidy through regular BBC broadcasts. The BBC approached Glyndebourne in 1934, but John Christie was insulted by the fees offered, and refused the opportunity. The following year, the offer was repeated, and raised; but Christie still refused. In 1936 he decided that the BBC's participation was desirable, and announced that the fees were still derisory but they could broadcast *Don Giovanni* free. Perhaps foolishly, the BBC found this unacceptable; and in due course fees were paid, though precisely what they were is not known. Rather than broadcast the whole of one opera, the BBC preferred separate evening relays of the first act of *Don Giovanni*, the first two acts of *Figaro*, and the second act of *Die Zauberflöte*. Local atmosphere was included to enhance the sense of occasion: the BBC put microphones among the trees to add birds, sheep and cows to the introductory presentation; and a real thunderstorm participated in *Figaro*. A dressing room served as the control room; and when it proved too reverberant, the hanging of some costumes in the middle of the room successfully damped the sound.

A year later, the BBC allowed listeners to hear Don Giovanni's fate, by broadcasting his second act, and also everything they had missed from *Die Zauberflöte*, plus the third act of *Figaro* and an act each of *Così fan tutte* and *Die Entführung*; by 1938 they were ready for the whole of *Figaro*, and two acts each of *Macbeth* and *Don Pasquale*. And there was a major breakthrough in presentation that year, when the announcer Frank Phillips was slipped into the producer's box in the theatre, so that announcements could be made between the scenes without the risk of speaking over music or holding up the performance.

Today these truncated broadcasts seem rather meagre, but it should be remembered that before the war the BBC had only two programmes (the National and the Regional), and that these live relays therefore overwhelmed the evening's schedule. For example the first complete *Figaro* began on the National programme with a leisurely 10-minute introduction at 6.40 p.m., and finished at 11.30 p.m. The shorter intervals were filled with unrelated talks, and the 75-minute dinner interval contained a selection from *Tannhäuser* on a cinema organ, News, Weather and a 30-minute play. After the war, the arrival of the Third Programme proved thoroughly advantageous to Glyndebourne, since it was possible to broadcast not only each opera complete but some operas more than once during the season, with a climax in 1954 during which 15 Glyndebourne performances (including those from Edinburgh) were broadcast within four months. Indeed, the BBC became so enamoured of Glyndebourne that in 1951 a series of weekend concerts was given in the theatre: Gui conducted the Royal Philharmonic Orchestra, Enesco the Boyd Neel, Pritchard the Philharmonia, and so on. And when the theatre was enlarged in 1953, the BBC was allowed to build a special control box at the back of the balcony. But Glyndebourne decided against encouraging outside parties to hire it as a venue. The festival occupied the best months of the year: during the other months, the place seemed cold, wet and windy, and it was not for nothing that the bar and foyer area surrounding the theatre became known as 'Pneumonia Way'.

Perhaps this most harmonious and favourable relationship between Glyndebourne and the BBC was too good to last. Or perhaps it was more to do with the overall development both of opera in Britain, and opera on the international broadcasting circuit. At any rate, the BBC began to reduce its Glyndebourne commitments in the 1960s, eventually settling for the present arrangement whereby each production might at the most be broadcast once. Glyndebourne was much consoled by William Glock's invitation to take part in the Proms, from 1961. The Prom appearances were carefully nurtured by Moran Caplat, who was determined that they should not be like any ordinary concert performances: the fact that the cast had sung perhaps some 12 performances should be regarded as a bonus, retaining of course the distinctive spirit of true ensemble. Caplat's efforts produced a tradition whereby the bones of the stage production are performed by the singers on a special stage; no sets or costumes are used, but each character is obliged to dress in something suitable for his or her role (obviously

Cherubino cannot be permitted to flounce around in pink chiffon and sequins), and a few props appear on the platform, usually with hilarious results. For those of a critical nature, these Glyndebourne Proms create an interesting opportunity to assess whether the musical performance is stronger or weaker without the personal fantasies of this or that stage producer and designer.

Television was born in Britain only two years after Glyndebourne itself; and when eventually television and opera discovered each other, much of the pioneer work was done by the BBC at Glyndebourne. There was considerable irony in this: the smallest theatre being made accessible to the largest of all audiences. Sadly, by the time the BBC first televised Glyndebourne in 1951, John Christie was too old to appreciate the full potential; but George Christie was allowed out of Eton to watch, and anxiously smoked a whole packet of Craven A cigarettes during the evening.

Not for the first or last time, the seeds were sown by the fact that a BBC executive happened to be a keen opera enthusiast. Cecil McGivern, Head of Television Programmes, saw Glyndebourne's production of *Così fan tutte* at Edinburgh in 1949. He visited Sussex the following season, and polite noises were made on both sides. The BBC had begun to be interested in opera on television in 1947, with performances from the Cambridge Theatre by the New London Opera Company; and by 1951 homespun studio productions in English (such as *La Bohème*, *La belle Hélène* and Menotti's *The Consul* and *The Telephone*) had become well established, receiving two live broadcasts each. But McGivern saw that Glyndebourne could offer better facilities for a different kind of production. At first, the small matter of fees nearly damned the whole thing. Caplat had to point out that what the BBC was offering would leave Glyndebourne with a loss of some £850 on the cost of giving the performance: the BBC seemed to think that Glyndebourne would be making a profit! In the end, the telecast was agreed at a cost to the BBC of £1,134, with Equity and the BBC agreeing a minimum chorus fee of 5 guineas plus 1 guinea for every day of rehearsal. Glyndebourne also managed to insist that Ebert, Busch and Caplat should have a power of veto over the television production. The BBC promised to pay for the 1,600 units of electricity used; and the mobile trans-mission van was parked on top of a nearby hill. Shortly before the big day, McGivern wrote to Caplat that he was convinced that, 'Glyndebourne and Television were born for each other and that, with care and thought on both sides, Television could be used to further the interests of Glyndebourne considerably.'

The BBC certainly did it properly. A special souvenir programme was printed. A distinguished audience in-vited by the BBC, including the Director General and the BBC's Governors, filled the theatre and enjoyed a VIP banquet. The cameramen wore tails; and although the weather did its best to drown the occasion, Peter Dimmock bravely performed the first of many pictur-esque introductions from the gardens. Thus the whole of Busch's last Glyndebourne performance of *Così fan tutte* was televised live, with a cast led by Jurinac as Fiordiligi, Lewis as Ferrando, and Bruscantini as Don Alfonso. Not only was the lighting drastically increased, but the production was revised so that the singers faced the cameras rather than the audience. Additional rehearsals were needed, provoking the first of many a disagreement between an opera orchestra and the BBC. The television critics were not much impressed, their reviews ranging from indignation to the cold, dismissive heading, 'Three Hours in Italian'. McGivern probably turned a blind eye to the viewing figures, which he never disclosed to Glyndebourne. He admitted that there had been too many long shots, making the singers look ridiculously small, and that the live interviews had been poor, with the exception of an inimitable performance by John Christie. But McGivern declared that, 'the whole thing was really most exciting and a milestone for us'; and his enthusiasm convinced everyone of the project's success. The only complaints came from the cast, which found waiting around during camera rehearsals tedious and tiring – a problem that has not diminished in thirty years.

Both parties then retired to their corners and reflected. John Christie was invariably against Glyndebourne being subjected to institutionalisation, but Caplat was extremely keen to repeat and expand the television potential. The BBC worried about its viewers. Perhaps an operetta in English might be a good idea for the next year; and maybe it should be done in the studio. Glyndebourne resisted. Then McGivern fell ill, and each side appreciated how much personal relationships had helped. By May 1952 the BBC and Glyndebourne had agreed that excerpts from *Macbeth* should be televised at the end of the season, and that the technical side should be more closely organised in advance.

They decided on three cameras, one tracking up a specially built ramp (which meant that a number of prime seats had to be blocked off as 'NBG'). The camera script was elaborately planned to include special effects for the witches and Banquo's ghost, superimposed by the third camera from back stage. Union agreements, or the lack of them, again threatened to jeopardise the project, but the BBC had no qualms about proposing that if Equity did not approve the dancers' fees (9 guineas for four days rehearsal and the performance), the ballet scenes would simply be cut. In the event, *Macbeth*, with what was considered an indifferent cast led by Marko Rothmüller and Dorothy Dow, but conducted by Gui, was a technical improvement on the previous effort.

McGivern told Glyndebourne that the viewing figures were about the same as for the previous year – but still did not say what sort of figures they were.

The BBC televised Glyndebourne every year from 1951 to 1967. Until 1966 the performance was always broadcast live, with the result that no recordings have survived. As with radio, in the early years, every opera was specially abridged for television. The selection was fairly conservative: *Die Entführung* in 1953, *Don Giovanni* in 1954, *Il barbiere di Siviglia* in 1955, and a Mozart selection for the bicentenary in 1956. Sometimes there were novel catastrophes, such as the camera staying so long on the climax of *Don Giovanni* that the villain and the Commendatore were seen to break the closing pose of clasped hands and slap each other on the back. Sometimes there were unusual pleasures, such as Oncina's Almaviva accompanying himself on the guitar. Often there were technical advances more memorable than much of what was still being done in the studio. Lionel Salter, Head of Music, Television, remembers that the 1956 excerpts from *Die Zauberflöte* included the first use of a high camera pan – slowly round the two armed men. Censorship reared its silly head in the case of the 1957 production of *Le Comte Ory*. Would BBC viewers be offended by Ory and his merry men dressing up as nuns? In the event, they were not; and the BBC was able to concentrate on more practical problems such as reducing the whiteness of the nuns' habits so that they did not upset the lighting levels.

Although the studio operas were still more adventurous in repertoire (several of them specially commissioned), it was quite a step for the BBC to televise *The Rake's Progress* from Glyndebourne in 1958. This was also the first opera to be televised complete from Glyndebourne – largely because nobody could think of how to cut it. To make things easier for the viewer, a spoken prologue was added; but afterwards everybody thought that it had sounded pretentious, so the BBC returned to the friendly informality of a presenter taken from within the company, such as Douglas Craig or later Peter Ebert. Meanwhile the audience grew rapidly, with *La cenerentola* receiving the first Eurovision relay in 1959. It was still a struggle to do a complete opera. In 1960 the BBC and Eurovision took all of *Falstaff* (with Geraint Evans in the title role) only because they could not decide whether to do the first two acts or the last two. In 1961 the BBC realised that sometimes it is an advantage to televise a production after the stage producer has lost touch with it. They were able to tone down Zeffirelli's production of *L'elisir d'amore* so that Mirella Freni was not disfigured by a silly wig; and (lest the audience complain about cruelty to animals) they dispensed with the donkey.

The BBC refused to let its commitment to opera be disturbed by the beginning of Independent Television in 1955. ITV started off boldly with a fortnightly concert by the Hallé Orchestra during peak viewing on Monday; all too soon this was reduced to only 30 minutes later in the evening, and ITV abandoned culture in favour of the view that 'what the public wants, it's going to get'. There were exceptions, such as Rediffusion's *Electra* in Greek in 1962; and there was the amazing phenomenon of Sydney Newman's 'Armchair Theatre' which in the late 1950s and early 1960s managed to do modern plays better than the BBC. But for the most part ITV merely watched the BBC's cultural heights, such as Glynde-bourne, with glee. For example, the 1964 relay of *Die Zauberflöte*, with a lengthy introduction by Peter Ebert, gave Rediffusion's current affairs programme 'This Week' (edited by Jeremy Isaacs) the best viewing figures in its entire history.

But as the 1960s progressed the BBC became unsure

of quite what it should be doing about opera – or rather Glyndebourne. There was so much on offer both from abroad (and the Eurovision exchanges cost virtually nothing) and from other British sources, especially after the BBC televised the Royal Opera for the first time, with excerpts from *Il trovatore* in 1965. The BBC demonstrated good faith in 1965 by asking Glyndebourne to stage three short operas specially for television after the season had ended: the 1954 production of *Arlecchino* sung in English; and a new double bill of *Dido and Aeneas* (with Janet Baker) and *L'Heure espagnole*. The arrangement worked well enough, but the following year Glyndebourne was shocked to learn that its festival offered nothing of interest to the BBC, in spite of the fact that the BBC was preparing to launch its second channel.

It was not that the Controller of BBC 2, David Attenborough, was against opera. The trouble was that the proposed production of Handel's *Jephtha* was well below Glyndebourne's best. Potted excerpts from *Werther* were suggested, without much enthusiasm; Glyndebourne wanted to do *La Bohème*, but the BBC had a studio production in progress. Glyndebourne and the BBC tried to establish a policy which could take into account the different requirements of BBC 1 and BBC 2. It was even suggested that each year Glyndebourne should do two operas in English for BBC 1, in addition to two of its own festival productions in the original language for BBC 2. Caplat's suggestion included an English version of the newly published Oeser edition of *Carmen*, and other shorter or less familiar operas such as de Falla's *La vida breve*, which he thought particularly suitable for television. Alas, nothing came of these proposals; and Glyndebourne probably felt somewhat aggrieved when BBC 2 opened in April 1967 with a live transmission of *La traviata* from the Royal Opera House, with Freni leading the cast and Giulini conducting Visconti's last London production. Later that year the BBC returned to Glyndebourne to make a television recording of the Enriquez production of *Don Giovanni*, the cast led by Kostas Paskalis, Paolo Montarsolo, Richard Lewis and Teresa Zylis-Gara. The overture was cut altogether; but the director, John Vernon, firmly claimed that the television audience did not complain.

For three years, the BBC wanted nothing from Glyndebourne. The BBC's new Head of Music and Arts, John Culshaw, was more interested in studio productions, which included the Britten operas from Aldeburgh and Basil Coleman's productions of *Otello* and *La vida breve*; the first opera in colour was a live *Aida* from the Royal Opera, in which Gwyneth Jones's make-up melted. The traditional Glyndebourne repertoire seemed to be all too easily available from perhaps less suitable sources, with a live *Così fan tutte* from the Royal Opera and a recording of *Don Giovanni* from Aix-en-Provence.

Though Glyndebourne had been the first outside broadcast with subtitles (Brian Dickie holding captions on postcards in front of a still camera), it missed out on significant improvements in subtitling. The first stage was the use of Letraset, with each letter painstakingly pressed on to a roll of paper by the present writer; next came the character generators which had to be superimposed manually; and finally the fully computerised systems which are programmed to the accuracy of 1/25th of a second. But it was back in the Letraset days of 1968 that Sir Huw Weldon said, 'I wish you'd subtitle *Peter Grimes*'.

The last of the Letraset subtitles marked the BBC's return to Glyndebourne in 1971, for Peter Hall's exquisite production of *La Calisto*, with Janet Baker revealing unexpected talents as a comic actress. This was Glyndebourne's first colour programme, and very pretty it was too. After one transmission the BBC appeared to have wiped or lost the master tape. Happily a copy has recently been discovered.

It was clear that the BBC and Glyndebourne had become bored with each other. Glyndebourne replied to its period of neglect with a salvo that surprised everyone: a contract with Southern Television. There was much talk of the importance of local patronage (and a generous management fee). Humphrey Burton, formerly Head of Music and Arts at the BBC, was borrowed from London Weekend Television to supervise this daring project; and Dave Heather, by no means experienced in music programmes, was invited to study the business of directing opera for television.

Southern Television did twelve operas at Glyndebourne in eight years. The quality varied. The first season's *Macbeth* seemed to be heading for disaster, beginning with Burton's rejection of Glyndebourne's Lady Macbeth in advance; in the end, Josephine Barstow took over the role, and gave an astonishing performance, and the old Enriquez production was vividly restaged by Michael Hadjimischev. Originally Southern intended to do all the Mozart operas, but they were caught between production cycles and it is arguable that their Mozart productions were less successful than the others such as the Hall–Leppard *Il ritorno d'Ulisse*, Ponnelle's *Falstaff*, the Cox–Hockney *Rake's Progress* and the Hall–Bury *Fidelio*. Meanwhile, it was rather provocative to have the BBC slipping back to do a delightful recording of Cox's production of *Capriccio* in 1976 (which many people considered the best of all Glyndebourne's television performances); they also returned for Peter Hall's charming new production of *Così fan tutte* in 1978, because Southern had done the old Enriquez production three years earlier. (It was during this BBC recording

147

that Peter Hall appeared to appreciate the special charms of the Dorabella of Maria Ewing. He slumped down in front of a monitor in the theatre, stared intently and said to me, 'She looks just like my first wife'.) But there was no doubt that Dave Heather and Southern were able to pay more attention to Glyndebourne during this period. Heather would spend all summer preparing his camera scripts, with special coaching on the text from Spike Hughes. Whereas the BBC was able to add only an odd puff of smoke to the transformation scenes in *La Calisto*, Southern would prepare and edit more liberally, with a bucket of water splashing upwards after the laundry basket dumped Falstaff into the river; there was also more fast cutting from one shot to another.

From Glyndebourne's point of view, Southern Television had one major disadvantage: it often proved difficult to get these recordings shown by the ITV network; and even when the transmission was eventually arranged, it was usually late at night, without the kind of publicity available to BBC programmes. Certainly the official audience was bigger; but was it a real opera audience, or just viewers who had gone to sleep with their sets still on? To everyone's surprise, in 1980 Southern lost its franchise to Television South, which intended to continue the agreement. In order to get the show on the road at short notice during that first summer, TVS simply used the old STV team led by Heather, for both the *Barbiere* production starring Maria Ewing and the enchanting Hall production of *Midsummer Night's Dream*. By 1982, however, the agreement was in a state of disarray. Though the advent of Channel 4 allowed far more opportunities for arts programmes from ITV companies, and Jeremy Isaacs was keen to make long-term arrangements as well as to show the programmes that ITV had failed to schedule, Glyndebourne decided that the time had come to return to the security of the BBC:

the Director-General himself had been making hopeful noises since the moment Southern lost its franchise. Crucial to the new BBC relationship were separate arrangements for world television and video rights.

The BBC returned in force in August 1983, recording three operas with different television directors. The experienced John Vernon was asked to cope with John Cox's elaborate production of *Cenerentola*, the most difficult to transpose to camera. One wit suggested that a special camera be ordered to correct the distorted perspectives of Allen Charles Klein's tables and chairs; Klein, like many theatrical people not accustomed to television work, hovered in the hinterland between tantrum and contract, especially when the electric generator operating the plastic chain of water for his dainty little fountain gave up just as the actual recording began. BBC 2 showed *Idomeneo* and *Intermezzo* a couple of months after recording, and saved *Cenerentola* for peak-time transmission on Christmas Day.

Idomeneo was particularly successful because Trevor Nunn himself worked on the camera script with the BBC's Christopher Swann (new to television opera, but not to Nunn as they had done a programme about *Cats* together). Glyndebourne's producers have often been present at television rehearsals, but pressure of time usually restricts them to minor adjustments and patient comments. ('All opera for television should be designed in black and white,' Peter Hall once sighed.) Nunn applied himself to every detail of the television adaptation with characteristic relish, restaging choruses, directing eyelines and asides, even vetting the subtitles by telephone from Vienna (and suggesting, 'I proclaim peace' for Idomeneo's 'Pace v'annunzio'). The final result combined visual simplicity and dramatic intensity, and set a standard for collaboration that Glyndebourne hopes to continue.

Back in the optimistic days of 1938, Christie and Bing planned to take Glyndebourne abroad as a *tour de force*; they never expected that a world war would mean that they were forced to tour. Plans for the 1940 festival were scrapped, and even a modest 'War Season', consisting of two weeks of *Figaro* and *Così fan tutte*, collapsed because Ebert was not available, neither were foreign singers. Glyndebourne was commandeered as a nursery school for 260 London children.

Soon an obvious course emerged: Glyndebourne should tour, with a British work, and a British cast. It was remembered that Ebert had once suggested staging *The Beggar's Opera* in the open air (coupled with Marlowe's *Faustus*) as a way of extending Glyndebourne's activities; it seemed an ideal choice in 1940, especially when Frederick Austin, who had arranged the music for the famous 1920 Playfair production, was found to be available. Strongly encouraged by Busch, a British cast was assembled around Audrey Mildmay as Polly and Roy Henderson as Peachum. Michael Redgrave played Macheath, Motley designed, John Gielgud produced. After six weeks at the Theatre Royal in Brighton, they toured Cardiff, Liverpool, Manchester, Glasgow, Edinburgh, and finished up at the Haymarket Theatre in London. The 4-month tour was not regarded as an artistic triumph, but it made a profit. A few weeks later, Audrey Mildmay and her children were evacuated to Canada for four years.

Naturally enough, John Christie was bursting with ideas as soon as war ended: a Wagner festival in London, at Drury Lane? Ernest Newman encouraged him, complaining that the new regime at Covent Garden seemed 'dead set on British artists, some of whom are more British than artists'. Nothing materialised until July 1946, and when it did, it was a far different project: the world première of Britten's *The Rape of Lucretia*. Britten and his colleagues were in retreat from the palace revolution that had upset the Sadler's Wells Opera two weeks before the première of *Peter Grimes*. They were now working on a chamber opera, but had neither funds nor theatre in which to stage it. Christie came to the rescue by making Glyndebourne available for *Lucretia*, providing one month of rehearsals and two weeks of performances there, after which the company toured London, the provinces and Holland. Glyndebourne's only artistic contribution was the suggestion of Kathleen Ferrier, who made her stage début as Lucretia. Britten's newly founded company, the English Opera Group, returned with *Albert Herring* in 1947, but Christie could not disguise his dislike of Britten's music, and would meet his guests with a gloomy face and comments such as, 'This isn't *our* kind of thing, you know'. The following year, Britten and his English Opera Group launched their first Aldeburgh Festival.

Glyndebourne's problem was simple: how to get going again, without costing Christie even more than in 1934. To partner the première of *Herring*, Glyndebourne assembled an Ebert production of Gluck's *Orfeo* with Kathleen Ferrier; but meanwhile Rudolf Bing had been busy on a more lasting solution. As soon as war ended, Bing had set his heart on organising a British festival of international calibre. Oxford was his first choice, but he could not find financial support; now he was to succeed in Edinburgh. (According to Glyndebourne legend, Audrey Mildmay had looked up at Edinburgh castle in the moonlight during the *Beggar's Opera* tour, and sighed that Edinburgh would make a wonderful setting for a festival.) As soon as Britten and his colleagues left Sussex, Bing brought a proper Glyndebourne company together to rehearse in Sussex, and then squash itself into the tiny King's Theatre as the first operatic event of the first Edinburgh Festival, on 25 August 1947.

Toscanini was asked to conduct *Macbeth* and Bruno Walter was offered *Figaro*. Both refused. Tullio Serafin was engaged for *Macbeth*, but the Inland Revenue scared him off; George Szell was engaged for *Figaro*, but fell out with the management and left during rehearsals. Glyndebourne's biggest success was the début of 37-year-old Giulietta Simionato as Cherubino; but Bing's ambitious festival, with Walter conducting the Vienna Philharmonic and soloists such as Schnabel, Szigeti, Primrose, Michelangeli and Fournier, got off to such a fine start that Glyndebourne lost its general manager to the full-time direction of the Edinburgh Festival. After three festivals, Bing moved to the Metropolitan Opera in New York, where he became the most autocratic manager of an artistic company since Diaghilev.

Bing made Glyndebourne an annual visitor to Edinburgh, and in 1948 and 1949 the company was able to reassert itself without risking performances in Sussex or any expense to Christie (who was still smarting over his 'startling' losses from the tour of *Lucretia*). Edinburgh was an exciting period. Glyndebourne was able to undertake a new production of *Così fan tutte* in 1948, with Ebert and Vittorio Gui working together for the first time since the war. *Don Giovanni* was revived, and the conductor Rafael Kubelik had the recitatives accompanied by the harpsichord for the first time in a Glyndebourne production. In 1949 the Royal Philharmonic Orchestra accompanied the company for the first time, and Ebert reproduced the famous production of *Un ballo in maschera*, designed by Caspar Neher, which he had done with Busch in Berlin in 1932.

Glyndebourne continued to visit Edinburgh annually for three weeks in the autumn; but 1951 was a peculiar year: the excellent success of *Idomeneo* in Sussex was not taken to Edinburgh; instead they took a new Busch–Ebert production of *La forza del destino* to mark the 50th anniversary of Verdi's death, without a single Italian in the cast; also a *Don Giovanni* that just went wrong. So it was not altogether surprising to hear that Bing's successor, Ian Hunter, had invited the Hamburg Opera to Edinburgh for 1952. Glyndebourne and its Scottish supporters were quite taken aback; angry letters were written to newspapers, reminding Mr Hunter that without Glyndebourne there would not have been an Edinburgh Festival.

Hunter subsequently invited Glyndebourne back for 1953, with *Cenerentola*, *Idomeneo* and the first British stage performance of *The Rake's Progress*; and again for two more years, although by this time the Sussex seasons were happily re-established. The year 1955 was vintage Edinburgh, with the new production of *Falstaff* conducted by Giulini (because Gui was ill). Edinburgh reporters relished the story of Osbert Lancaster including a grotesque Lady Godiva on a hobby horse in the final scene in Windsor forest, leading to John Christie's announcement that he was directly descended from the lady in question. (Did Edinburgh have such fun with German companies?) After that, Glyndebourne stayed in Sussex, Edinburgh invited companies from abroad. There was one return, in 1960, when they revived *Falstaff* with Geraint Evans in his prime in the title role, and took the new Sussex production of *I puritani* with Joan Sutherland. When John Drummond became Edinburgh's festival director and temporarily abandoned foreign companies, the idea of Glyndebourne's return in the 1980s was briefly discussed; times had changed, and it did not seem a good idea for either side.

Glyndebourne still flirted with the notion of touring abroad. Hurok made hopeful noises about an American tour in 1952; but lack of money defeated all hopes, as usual. Christie tried all sources, even the British Council which, he suggested, could help with transport by sending Glyndebourne abroad in British ships. When Sir Ronald Adam protested that one of the reasons for the Council's lack of interest was that Glyndebourne sang in Italian and German, Christie's indignation was unbounded: such a petty, chauvinistic attitude, regardless of excellence, 'gives me ammunition for my Crusade. My team will not be daunted.'

At last, in 1954, Glyndebourne made its first trip abroad; but so modestly. Carl Ebert had just returned (after an absence of 21 years) to the Städtische Oper in what had become West Berlin; he invited Glyndebourne to give two performances of *Cenerentola* there, and the result was a triumph from every point of view, including the number of curtain calls. Then there was the extraordinary Liverpool season of 1956, when it transpired that Glyndebourne would not be going to Edinburgh in September. The Liverpool Philharmonic Society invited Glyndebourne to play for two weeks at the Royal Court Theatre, with the Liverpool Philharmonic: Gui and John Pritchard shared the performances. Such was the success of this venture that Moran Caplat almost out-Christied the absent (and ageing) Christie himself: Glyndebourne would buy an old aircraft carrier, and turn it into an opera ship, touring the great cities of the world by sea, with a 350-seat auditorium, luxurious restaurants, etc. Ah well! Glyndebourne went to Paris in 1958, and to Scandinavia in 1967. But for all the genuine pleasure and excitement of these tours, as the years passed one thing became overwhelmingly clear. It was hard enough to assemble good casts for the festival's own season; trying to keep them together for touring as well was virtually impossible. Today George Christie is quite blunt about it: 'It's got to be for a *lot* of money, or a *lot* of prestige – preferably both. Otherwise, so far as the festival is concerned, it's not worth it.'

Meanwhile, like a pair of spectacles that cannot be

found because it is already upon your nose, the means through which Glyndebourne could expand had been obvious since 1935: understudies. Being a seasonal organisation, Glyndebourne had always been able to keep its chorus young, fresh, talented; and it was from the chorus that all the understudies were drawn, and coached to Glyndebourne standards in major roles during both the rehearsal period and the festival itself. But they hardly ever had a chance to go on. As Busch put it in 1935, 'No stars are ever away at Glyndebourne, because even work is more attractive than the night life of Lewes'. By the 1960s the frustration of the Glynde-bourne understudy had become familiar enough to provoke a party joke in which, after twenty years of patient waiting, an understudy goes into the Covered Way and cries, 'Last bus for Lewes station'.

The Glyndebourne management also found the waste distressing, especially when a role learnt at Glynde-bourne was subsequently sung with great success at Sadler's Wells or Covent Garden. The idea of a second eleven grew gradually, beginning with the custom of giving understudy performances, rather like auditions, to members of the management and company. Not every-body was in favour of a second eleven: Moran Caplat feared that it would spoil the first eleven's pitch. But when George Christie assumed more responsibility after his father's death in 1962, the things which naturally concerned him as a member of a younger, perhaps less élite generation, were not only the languishing under-studies but also the desirability of making Glyndebourne available to a wider, younger, less rich audience. There was also the fact that Glyndebourne's resources – sets, costumes, wigs, and their attendant personnel – were lying idle for an unnecessarily large part of the year.

Providence encouraged the idea during 1965, when a relatively large number of festival principals fell sick,

and the understudies did particularly well. By the end of
that season George Christie's plans were far enough
advanced for him to announce the development of 'a
Glyndebourne Touring Group' during his traditional
speech on the last night. *The Times* published a leading
article which applauded Glyndebourne for having 'a social
conscience as well as an artistic one', but warned that 'like
the Sadler's Wells touring company and the English Opera
Group, they will not find audiences ready-made. Part of
Glyndebourne's drawing power has always lain in the
prospect of a pleasant summer-time journey to the Sussex
Downs, eating one's sandwiches overlooked by cows . . .'

Finding the money was a major problem, but
Glyndebourne had good friends. The Arts Council was
strongly in favour of the idea, and gave £29,000 for the
first six-week tour. Before his father died, George
Christie had worked for the Gulbenkian Foundation,
which favoured grants for special purposes rather than
everyday running costs; to help get the project launched,
they committed £15,000 for the first year, £10,000 for the
second; £5,000 for the third; and Sir Bernard Miller,
head of the John Lewis Partnership (an invaluable friend
of Glyndebourne), did his best to mobilise the provincial
business community. Getting money from local au-
thorities was a task that drained more energy from the
applicant than pennies from rate-payers; some were
'generous', others 'conspicuously mean'. The first tour,
with four operas in six cities, cost £80,000; after all
tickets had been sold and grants scrounged, Glyndebourne itself was left with a loss of just over £3,000. In
1983 the cost of touring three operas for seven weeks is
estimated at a little over £¾m. After subsidy, sponsorship and the best auditing figures forecast for any British
touring company, there is still a loss of about £50,000 to
be borne by Glyndebourne.

The touring company was set up as an operation

separate from the festival, but both of its principal figures emerged from within Glyndebourne. Brian Dickie, who became the administrator, had joined Glyndebourne in the job known locally as 'carrying Jani's* satchel'. (This required arranging all the music calls and rehearsal schedules, and has proved an outstanding training for higher things; Dickie rose to General Administrator of the festival itself; his immediate successor, Nicholas Snowman, founded the London Sinfonietta with David Atherton and was then swept off to Paris by Boulez to run IRCAM, the contemporary music organisation in the Pompidou Centre.) The choice of principal conductor was easy, since at that time the festival had a particularly good chorus master, Myer Fredman: young and energetic, and capable of managing a wide repertoire.

They chose to open in Newcastle, in March 1968, because it was from that city that the touring orchestra had been selected: the Northern Sinfonia. And right from the beginning, GTO was obliged to face the eventfulness of a travelling company's life – or to put it more realistically, the wretched facilities of touring. Fredman had to stack five chairs on top of each other in order to rehearse the Northern Sinfonia at Jesmond. Meanwhile, sets and costumes for four productions were crammed into a convoy of furniture vans and one small articulated lorry. The schedule was hectic: leave Sussex on Saturday, arrive Newcastle on Sunday, open on Monday. (By 1982 GTO was leaving Sussex in ten large articulated lorries.) Few provincial theatres have a stage as deep as Glyndebourne's 60 feet, so it has been common for sets to be cut down (although great pains have been taken not to savage anything painted by David Hockney); and sometimes the access to the

*Jani Strasser, Head of Music Staff from 1934 to 1970.

backstage area has been so tight that large props have been cut into pieces and then reassembled inside. Moving from one city to another has also created problems: a force 10 gale in March 1968 prevented the lorries from crossing the Pennines en route from Newcastle to Liverpool, so the sets of *Zauberflöte* arrived only just before the audience, and the lighting was improvised during the performance, very little of it making contact with the Queen of the Night.

Such accidents are inherent in touring, but at first, for a company nursed at Glyndebourne, it seemed a far cry from the smooth professionalism of the Sussex season. Orchestral parts needed in Newcastle were found at midday under the stage in Oxford, 250 miles away; they arrived by taxi two minutes before the curtain was due to rise. In Manchester they ran out of programmes, so the company manager told the story of *Eugene Onegin* over the tannoy, only to be thanked by one of the programme sellers with the words, 'Ee, that was luvly. Just like "Listen with Mother"'. The Sheffield stage was so oddly raked that Luzzati's moving columns kept falling over during the Saturday matinee of *Zauberflöte*; and a Tamino who ran out of voice after the first scene had to be replaced in the middle of the act by his understudy without a moment in which to disguise the fact that one tenor was white and the other coloured.

Local newspapers have supported GTO enthusiastically, but not always to the point. Publicity for the first tour was almost overwhelmed by the donkey required for *L'elisir d'amore*. Local beasts – such as Ringo, Toby and Jennie – were auditioned to the delight of photographers and the neglect even of GTO's most delectable singers. But the last donkey, an Oxford lad, became such a favourite that Brian Dickie gave him as a wedding present to his secretary, and he now lives a busy and fecund life at stud in Cumberland (the donkey, not

Dickie). The company has gradually been obliged to recognise certain facts about regional audiences. Oxford is by far GTO's best attended week, especially when less popular operas are being toured. *Don Giovanni* and *Figaro* are operas that can be toured in consecutive years; *Falstaff* cannot.

The musical accomplishment of GTO is too rich and varied to list in detail here; enough to say, in general, that it has become a major element in the developing operatic life of the provinces; more artistically successful and financially secure, surely, than several of the major provincial companies themselves. Perhaps it is contradicting the ensemble spirit of the company to list individual singers, but an idea of the calibre of talent can easily be given by recalling that the 1968 tour had Jill Gomez and Ryland Davies in *L'elisir*; and in those early years Richard Van Allan was the regular Mozart buffo, with Leporello, Osmin and Don Alfonso. By the beginning of the 1970s the company had settled down and was fielding Elizabeth Gale as Blonde, Susanna and Nanetta; Benjamin Luxon as Onegin; Linda Esther Gray as Mimi, the Countess in *Figaro*, Tatyana in *Onegin* and Agathe in *Freischütz*. That generation was followed by Lillian Watson as Despina and Susanna; Felicity Lott as Fiordiligi and the Countess in *Capriccio*; Rosalind Plowright as Elvira and the Countess in *Figaro*; John Rawnsley as Ford in *Falstaff* and Nick Shadow in *Rake's Progress*; Jonathan Summers as Falstaff; and Thomas Allen as Don Giovanni. Sometimes the most daunting challenge, such as singing *Orfeo* after Janet Baker's operatic farewell in the 1982 festival, has been met by a GTO performance which not only introduces an outstanding young singer (in this case, Carolyn Watkinson, quite different both in vocal colour and dramatic character) but also reaches an overall distinction that has made it seem worthy of the festival itself.

Destination Glyndebourne

John Julius Norwich

My first experience of Glyndebourne was not an un-
qualified success. It was a long time ago now, soon after
the end of the war, and I was on leave from National
Service in the Navy, spending a few days with some
friends in Norfolk. Early one Sunday morning, the
telephone rang. It was my mother, who had just been
offered two tickets for *Così fan tutte* that same afternoon.
Could I be at Glyndebourne by four-thirty? Of course I
could, I said brightly, and hung up.

Little did I know how fateful those words were. The
ABC revealed one slow Sunday train, leaving in an
hour's time from a station fifteen miles away. Fortunately it was late or I should never have caught it; and it was a
good deal later still when it finally crawled into Liverpool
Street. A mood of relative serenity during the early
stages of the journey had long since given way to one of
anguish. There was only one possible connection to be
made; in normal circumstances I should have had over an
hour to get from Liverpool Street to Victoria, but I now
realised that I had exactly twenty minutes. Mercifully it

was a Sunday afternoon, and there was a waiting taxi. I offered the driver double fare if we made it. He looked gloomy, but his practical response was magnificent. We hurtled across London, and arrived at Victoria with a minute to spare. There was just time to hurl my suitcase and myself into the last, rapidly-accelerating carriage and to fall, half-dead but happy, into an empty seat.

We were among green fields before I had recovered sufficiently to size up my fellow-travellers. There were two ladies bedecked, as I remember, in yards of mauve chiffon, looking like large, flustered moths. Only at the ankles did the chiffon stop, to give place to intricate systems of gold and silver strapping. Their escorts wore stiff collars, winged like archangels; one of them sported one of those square, single-breasted black evening waistcoats, now found only on the older and seedier waiters in French provincial cafés. Suddenly I became conscious of an almost tangible atmosphere of disapproval: I was an outsider, an intruder. I had forced myself upon their company and in doing so had cheapened both myself and them. Sartorially, I was letting down the side.

A terrible thought struck me. I was only eighteen and had spent the last three years abroad; but had I not heard somewhere that at Glyndebourne evening dress was *de rigueur*? Perhaps without it I should be refused admittance, bringing disgrace upon my mother and rendering pointless this whole ghastly journey. With relief I remembered that my dinner jacket was in my suitcase. I would brave the disapproval a little longer; then I would betake myself and suitcase along the corridor and emerge on Lewes station metamorphosed.

Twenty minutes before our scheduled arrival time I was locked safely in the loo, stripped to my underpants and unbuttoning a clean white shirt, when suddenly the train stopped. I could see nothing through the frosted glass, but I heard, all too clearly, a voice of genteel doom: 'Brighton, this is Brighton. The special train for Glyndebourne leaves in three minutes from platform six. Brighton, this is Brighton . . .'

I felt like Job, or Titus Andronicus. When would this fearful slumber have an end? No one had told me that we had to change trains. (Admittedly, they hadn't had much of a chance.) Speed, by now, was a good deal more important than elegance, even than decency; still, I could hardly chase across Brighton station in the middle of a Sunday afternoon clad only in my underpants. Shirt, trousers and shoes, seemed the best compromise. Stuffing everything else hugger-mugger into the suitcase, I fled down the platform – remembering only at the barrier that I had no ticket. There was no time to explain; neither, however, was there any need to. The ticket collector, after one astonished look, instinctively knew that his duty was to see me either on to the Glyndebourne train or to the nearest police station. He took – I gratefully record it – the right decision. Leaving his barrier unattended, he seized the suitcase and hustled me to platform six. A colleague held out his hand for my ticket, but was impatiently waved aside. The train was already grunting itself into motion. Doors were banging, flags were waving. This, I realised, was not only a nightmare, it was a recurring nightmare. I had done all this before, only this time I was half-naked. It is not easy to jump into a moving train when one hand is holding up one's trousers, but I made it.

The last stage of the journey was the worst. This time there was no empty seat, just eight more passengers, obviously from the same stable as the other lot, all looking like something out of an H.M. Bateman cartoon – shocked, horrified and personally affronted. I could think only of escape – down the corridor again. But this time there was no corridor. I was trapped – and at bay.

With what little power of speech remained, I tried to explain the situation; and then the miracle happened. They all started to laugh. Better still, they helped. A gentleman took my suitcase and held it open on his knees. A lady raised aloft a tiny mirror while I tied my tie. Somebody else held me steady in the lurching train while I put on my socks. By the time we reached Lewes I was, I think, relatively presentable. I thanked them all, but not enough. If any of them read this, I hope they will take it as a renewed expression of gratitude.

It had been raining in Norfolk, but at Glyndebourne the sun was blazing down, and my recent passage through hell sharpened my appreciation of paradise. All that I had ever heard about the place suddenly came together, in focus for the first time. Members of the orchestra were playing croquet. Bottles of champagne were being cooled in the lake. In a distant dressing-room, a tenor was warming up with a few arpeggios. Even the mauve chiffon and the wing collars had lost their terrors for me; they were no longer formidable, but festive. Almost regretfully, we left the golden afternoon outside and trooped into the theatre. Fritz Busch raised his baton and one magic spell gave place to another. Mesdames Jurinac and Thebom gave what I still feel must have been the performances of their lives. It was my first *Così*, and for me it has never been surpassed.

But how many memorable Glyndebourne treats there have been since! My mind goes back to that glorious *Idomeneo* with the Oliver Messel sets; to the *Rake's Progress* in which, by a stroke of sheer inspiration, the genius of Stravinsky was combined with that of Osbert Lancaster; to Raymond Leppard's *Calisto*; and to another incandescent evening in (I think) 1953 when, with *Ariadne auf Naxos*, I was first knocked sideways by that most dazzling of all operatic partnerships, Hugo von Hofmannsthal and Richard Strauss. For these, and a

hundred others that I might just as easily have mentioned, I am more grateful than I can say. Little did I
suspect what a long, sumptuous and infinitely satisfying
succession of delights was opening out before me as I
pelted, in such desperate *déshabille*, down the Brighton
platform thirty-five years ago.

Index

Index

Index

Index